Economic Decision Making Using Cost Data

Economic Decision Making Using Cost Data

A Manager's Guide

Daniel Marburger and Ryan Peterson

First published in 2013 by
Business Expert Press, LLC
222 East 46th Street, New York, NY 10017
www.businessexpertpress.com

ISBN-13: 978-1-60649-512-4 (paperback)
ISBN-13: 978-1-60649-513-1 (e-book)

Business Expert Press Economics collection

Collection ISSN: 2163-761X (print)
Collection ISSN: 2163-7628 (electronic)

Cover and interior design by Exeter Premedia Services Private Ltd.
Chennai, India

First edition: 2013

10 9 8 7 6 5 4 3 2 1

Printed in the United States of America.

Abstract

A firm maximizes profits if each decision adds more to the firm's revenue than to its costs. Although the concept sounds rather simple, it is difficult to do in practice. Economic theory helps the decision-maker to accurately infer changes in revenues that may be associated with a decision. Similarly, economic theory suggests that the costs reported by accountants rarely reflect the true cost associated with the decision. The purpose of this book is to help managers understand how to assess the changes in revenues and costs. Demand and price sensitivity analysis allow managers to infer revenue changes. This book also reconciles the economic theory of cost with common accounting practices so the differences can be reconciled and better decisions can be made.

Keywords

absorption costing, activity-based costing, cost allocation, demand analysis, direct and indirect costs, fixed and variable costs, marginal cost, opportunity cost, unit cost, price elasticity, relevant costs, relevant revenues, variable costing.

Contents

Contents

List of Firms/Products

Chapter 1

1. Indian Mall
2. Mercator Minerals

Chapter 2

1. Enron
2. Blockbuster

Chapter 3

1. Netflix
2. National Association for Convenience Stores
3. Orbitz
4. Toyota and Honda
5. Apple Corporation
6. Burger King
7. Proctor and Gamble

Chapter 5

1. Financial Accounting Standards Board
2. Anvil Farms

Chapter 6

1. Parker Hannifin
2. Rockwell International

Preface

The purpose of this book is to help managers make better decisions. Balance sheets and income statements reflect the results of past decisions. They do not evaluate individual decisions, nor do they provide definitive insights into decisions the firm may undertake in the future. But maximizing the value of the firm only occurs if each *individual* decision adds to its profits. Therefore, the manager must focus on the revenues and costs that will change if a decision is implemented.

Take, for example, a simple pricing decision. A manager is asked to quote a price to a prospective customer who may purchase up to three units. He realizes that if his quote is too high, he will lose the order to a competitor. If his quote is too low, the profit from the transaction may be inadequate. The firm could even incur a loss if the quote is too low. To make the proper quote, the manager may rely on prices quoted on previous orders or the prices quoted by competing firms on lost orders. The manager must also consult unit cost estimates passed along by cost accountants.

Let's assume that the unit cost estimate is $700. The manager logically assumes that each unit of output costs $700 to produce. Hence, the manager could not quote a price below $700 without incurring a loss. But in a recent request for proposal, the unit cost estimate was also $700 and the firm lost the order to a competitor that quoted $680. How could that have happened? Is the competitor more efficient? Does it have a cheaper supplier of raw materials? Is it incurring a short-term loss as part of a larger strategic initiative? Or is it simply guilty of bad decision making?

Perhaps the fault lies with the cost accountant? He has an accounting degree, but maybe he's careless. Is he allocating costs improperly, causing the firm to lose orders?

In all likelihood, the competitor is *not* more efficient, does *not* have a cheaper supplier, and is *not* incompetent. Nor is cost accounting likely to be the source of the problem. The cost accountant is probably using widely accepted practices and there is nothing inherently suspect in the numbers. Furthermore, it is quite likely that the manager from the competing firm has unit cost estimates that are very nearly the same as this firm. So what gives?

The answer may be embedded in economic theory. Economic theory provides insights that can help a manager make better decisions. Consumer choice theory describes the underpinnings of demand, which is the essence of pricing and purchasing behavior. Under what circumstances does the manager need to match the competitor's price? Is it possible to land the order with a price that is higher than those quoted by competitors? When can the firm undercut the competitor's price and *still* lose the order? Similarly, production and cost theory provide the basis for understanding unit cost. If the unit cost estimate is $700, is it logical to assume that each unit costs $700 to produce?

One major insight that emanates from economic theory is that unit cost estimates do not necessarily reflect the actual cost of each individual unit. This does not imply that the cost accountant has done anything wrong or that a new method of accounting would provide more accurate estimates. Rather, economic theory suggests that each unit of output has its own unique cost: the cost of producing the first unit differs from the cost of producing the second unit, which differs from producing the 1,276th unit. It would be prohibitively expensive, and in fact, it may be impossible for cost accounting to adopt a method that would accurately measure the cost of producing each individual unit. For this reason, cost accounting methods estimate *average* unit costs over ranges of output as the best available estimate for the cost of an individual unit.

But if the unit cost estimate is an average, is it possible that the actual unit cost figure is higher or lower than the estimated figure? This is clearly important because the manager relies on these estimates in quoting a price in our example. If the difference between the estimated and actual unit costs was due to random error, the manager could still rely on them because the actual unit cost is equally likely to be underestimated or overestimated.

In fact, however, unit costs are expected to follow patterns described by economic theory. This could result in unit cost estimates that *systematically* over- or underestimate actual unit cost over a given range of production. This can best be shown by going back to our original example. Recall that a prospective customer is considering purchasing up to three units and wants the manager to quote a price. Cost accounting supplies a unit cost estimate of $700, so the manager sets a price of $750. This implies a profit of $50/unit, or a total profit of $150.

But suppose theory suggests that the cost of producing each individual unit is rising. Specifically, the cost of producing the first unit is $600, the cost of producing the second unit is $700, and the cost of producing the third unit is $800. The cost accountant was correct in asserting that the average cost of producing three units is $700. But the manager incorrectly inferred that *each* unit costs $700 to produce. Consequently, the firm spent $800 to produce the third unit while selling it for only $750. Again, our contention is not that the cost accountant erred, or that there is a better way to estimate unit costs. Rather, because it is impossible to devise a system that accurately imputes the cost of producing individual units, the cost accountant did the next best thing: supplying a unit cost estimate that is, in fact, an average. Nonetheless, the manager's failure to reconcile unit cost estimates with the economic theory of cost resulted in underpricing the third unit.

Suppose unit cost is constant across all three units. If this is the case, the manager can quote a price of $750 without fear of underpricing. But we stated that the firm lost the order to a competitor that quoted $680. Does the competitor have lower unit costs or is it destined to lose money at the winning quote? Quite conceivably, the answer is neither. Assume both firms have identical cost structures. The manufacturing plants for both firms produce multiple goods and the respective cost accountants follow the common practice of allocating the production supervisor's salary as part of the unit cost estimate. Suppose the allocated salary comprises $50 of the unit cost estimate. What happens to the plant supervisor's salary if the firm gets the order? Presumably, nothing. If not, then if the firm lands the order, its expenses will rise by $650/unit, not $700/unit. This means the firm that quoted a price of $680 made the right decision, and the manager who was reluctant to quote a price below $700 for fear of losing money missed out on a chance to land a profitable order.

This book was co-authored by an economist and an accountant to fill a perceived gap in most managerial economics and managerial accounting textbooks. Few economists are schooled in cost accounting. Managerial economics textbooks invariably assume that managers know the cost of producing each and every unit. But they don't, and it's unrealistic to assume that they do. At the same time, few accounting textbooks teach the economic theory of cost. Most texts concentrate on implementation: how to estimate unit cost using commonly accepted methods. The fact that it is impossible for the unit cost estimates to accurately reflect actual unit cost is rarely mentioned; yet it is critical to managerial decisions.

This is the niche that our book seeks to fill. Managers need to make decisions that will increase the firm's profits. In doing so, the manager must anticipate the amount by which revenues will rise if the decision is implemented as well as the amount by which costs will increase. These are referred to as *relevant revenues* and *relevant costs*. Economic theory provides valuable insights that will help managers anticipate relevant revenues and costs. Moreover, theory helps to reconcile the economic theory of cost with the inherently imperfect estimates supplied by cost accounting. Different cost accounting methods provide different unit cost estimates and can bias decision making in different ways. Anticipating the difference between the unit cost estimate and actual unit cost can lead to better decisions.

Who should read this book? Our primary target audience is business managers who make decisions that utilize unit cost estimates. They must understand various cost accounting methods and the economic theory of cost and anticipate the likely difference between estimated and actual unit cost. They need to know how misunderstanding the unit cost estimate may lead to poor decisions.

A secondary target audience consists of practicing cost accountants. This is not a "how-to-do-it" accounting text. We assume that accountants who purchase this book already know how to implement absorption, variable, or activity-based costing. However, this book lends unique insights as to how cost accounting practices result in estimates that differ from the numbers they seek to measure.

CHAPTER 1

What Does Economics Have to Do with Running a Business?

What Is Economics All About?

Mention the word "economist" and one conjures up a vision of an academic who scours over macroeconomic data and utilizes sophisticated statistical techniques to make forecasts. Indeed, many economists do just that. But some people may be surprised to learn that economics is a social science, not a business science. Like psychology, sociology, anthropology, and the other social sciences, economics studies human behavior. That includes consumer behavior, firm behavior, and the behavior of markets.

Economic theory is mired in simple logic. We assume people pursue a goal and things get in the way. How they deal with the constraints is the discipline of economics. Consider a simple example. A manager in Milwaukee has to call on a client in downtown Chicago. One way to get to Chicago from Milwaukee is to get on I-94 and drive south to downtown Chicago. The distance is 90 miles and the trip should take two hours. This is not the only way to get to Chicago. An alternative is to take I-94 west to Madison, take I-39 south to I-80, go east until I-94, and then go due north until he reaches downtown Chicago. The alternative route will cover 310 miles and take five-and-a-half hours to complete. Given a choice, economists predict he'll take the 90-mile, two-hour route.

You are unlikely to be impressed with this prediction, but it is the essence of economics. The manager's goal is to reach Chicago. We assume the manager values his free time and would rather not spend it driving. If he had it his way, he'd snap his fingers and he'd be in Chicago. But this is not an option. Wanting to use up as little free time as possible, he scouts out all available routes. If the manager travels to Chicago via the direct route, he foregoes two hours of free time. If he travels by way of Madison, he gives up five-and-a-half hours of free time. Because he cannot eliminate the constraint, his objective is to reach Chicago and forego as little free time as possible. This is why he chooses the direct route.

The theory of the firm is similar. Economists typically assume the goal of your firm is to maximize profits. However, your business must deal with constraints. You are going to need workers to produce your good. Because wages paid to employees reduce the firm's profits, you want to pay them as little as possible. How much, at a minimum, must you pay them? If an individual works for you, he cannot work for someone else at the same time. Therefore, if you want to hire a worker, you must offer a salary that's at least as good as what he can get from another employer.

Your firm will also require raw materials to produce the good. Payments to suppliers mean less profit for the firm. You want to pay them as little as necessary. How much must they be paid? Any item the suppliers sell to you cannot be sold to someone else. If you want their business, you must offer a price that's at least as attractive as what they can get from another firm.

Notice the parallel between the firm and the manager who needs to go to Chicago. The distance between Milwaukee and Chicago is 90 miles. The manager can do nothing to shorten this distance, so he tries to deal with it by taking the most direct route he can. The firm cannot hope to attract workers or raw materials without compensation. The cheapest means to secure the necessary labor and materials is to pay them what they're worth to competing firms.

Beyond production costs, the firm's profits are also constrained by the options available to the consumers. Consumers don't have to buy the good from your firm. They can buy it from another firm. They can decide not to buy the good at all. If you want consumers to buy from you, you must offer a good at a price/quality that is commensurate with what they can get from other firms.

There are innumerable obstacles that can get in the way of profitability, and economists dedicate themselves to studying how profit-seeking firms deal with these constraints. And that's what economics has to offer the business manager. Managers have to deal with the threat of competition, legal constraints, changing consumer tastes, a complex, evolving labor force, and a myriad of other obstacles. The essence of economics is to determine how to deal with the forces of nature that get in the way of the firm's goals.

The Role of Opportunity Cost

The most important concept in economics is *opportunity cost.* For any action one takes, he foregoes alternatives. If you stay late at the office, you may miss an opportunity to see your daughter's piano recital. You may miss a football game on television. You may miss an opportunity for a good home-cooked meal. To justify working late, the value of the extra time at the office must exceed the alternative on which you place the most value. You may consider the additional work to be more important than either the football game or the home-cooked meal. But unless it is also more important than the piano recital, you will not work late. Opportunity cost is the highest valued alternative foregone. On many days, you might be able to leave the work until the next morning. If so, the value of working late is relatively small, allowing you to attend the recital. However, you may have to meet a critical deadline. If this is the case, the value of staying late at the office may exceed the value of the recital. In either circumstance, opportunity cost plays a role in your decision. Because the recital is the most important of all foregone activities, you will not work late unless the value of staying at the office exceeds the highest valued alternative foregone.

If you review the previous discussion, you'll see opportunity cost pop up over and over. If an employee works for your firm, he cannot work for another firm during the same hours. Consequently, if you don't offer enough money, he will work for someone else. If a supplier of industrial equipment sells a machine to you, it cannot sell the exact same machine to another firm. Thus, if you aren't willing to pay a price that's commensurate with what other firms are paying, the supplier won't sell the good to you. If a consumer purchases from you at a given price, he cannot spend the money on other goods he values. If you don't offer a good that offers an overall value that is competitive with what other firms are charging, the consumer will not buy from you. Therefore, opportunity cost dictates the wage you pay, the price you pay to suppliers, and the price you charge for your product.

Opportunity costs should be distinguished from payments. When a student enrolls in college, his opportunity cost is not simply what he could have purchased with his tuition money. It also includes the foregone income from having a full-time job and the free time he gives up by studying late at night.

Opportunity costs should also not be confused with past expenses. Decisions are always forward looking; hence, opportunity cost refers to the highest valued alternative foregone if the firm takes a given action. As an example, suppose you want to entertain clients at a baseball game and you buy three nonrefundable tickets for $50 each. As you meet outside the gate, you learn that one of the clients had to cancel at the last minute. Rather than throw the ticket away, you sell it to a scalper for $30. The historical cost of the ticket was $50. On paper, you lost $20. However, because the ticket was nonrefundable, you found yourself with two choices: throw it away or sell it for $30. By selling it to the scalper, you're $30 better off than your next best alternative.

Let's reiterate this point again: because decisions are always forward thinking, the opportunity cost associated with the decision should not be equated with past expenses. But this is precisely what cost accountants do. They record the cost of a transaction *after the decision has been made*. The firm purchases raw materials and the cost of the transaction is recorded. As partially completed units flow through departments, additional costs are logged as they are incurred. When the units are sold, the accountant records the cost of goods sold. At no time does the accountant record the opportunity cost of a future decision. Rather, he logs the historical cost of decisions that have already been made.

If unit costs are recorded in historical terms, but opportunity costs are forward thinking, what is the value of unit cost estimates? To understand, consider the ramifications of having no cost estimates. With each decision, the manager would have to undergo a search for all relevant information that might allow him to assess opportunity cost. Unit cost estimates provide a benchmark that substitute for a lot of inefficient searching. Although cost-accounting estimates should not be equated with opportunity cost, they serve as a useful starting point for assessing opportunity cost.

Opportunity cost plays a critical role in capital budgeting decisions. Suppose a firm is considering purchasing an expensive piece of machinery that is likely to reduce unit costs by 10% over its useful life. The firm is considering financing the purchase out of its retained earnings. Is it worthwhile? The cost of capital used to determine net present value represents the opportunity cost of the purchase. If the firm does not buy the machinery, the money could be distributed to stockholders as dividends. The stockholders may be willing to forego the dividends if they believe the cost savings will yield an even greater benefit to them in the future. The cost of capital should reflect the return stockholders require in exchange for foregoing dividends.

For example, in 2012, Mercator Minerals completed a feasibility study for the potential development of a large-scale, low-cost copper mine in northern Mexico. To evaluate the investment, the firm relied on a cost of capital of 8%, implying that its investors required a minimum return of 8% to justify the venture. Based on an estimated mine life of 13 years, the analysis determined that the project would increase the firm's after-tax wealth by $417 million over and above the earnings that could have been generated by simply investing the funds in a portfolio with an annual yield of 8%.[1]

Economic Theory in Decision Making

Let's use an applied example to illustrate the value of economic theory in decision making. In 1967, the college town of Jonesboro, Arkansas, built the Indian Mall. As Jonesboro was the commercial hub of northeast Arkansas, the Indian Mall was "the place to shop" for 40 years. The town nearly doubled in size over the next few decades, and in 2006, a new mall, the Mall at Turtle Creek, opened for business. The shift of shoppers from the old mall to the new one was immediate and significant. At many Indian Mall stores, customer traffic was half of what it had been the year before.[2] Some stores closed their doors immediately, whereas others remained open until their leases expired. The mall officially closed in February 2008 and was demolished four years later.

Let's use this example to examine strategic decision making. The businesses leasing space at the Indian Mall knew that the exodus of customers was permanent. Why did most stores close their doors immediately, whereas others remained open? Quite conceivably, some firms may have decided to close their doors because they were losing money and had no chance of making a profit. Why did some stores remain open? If customer traffic had fallen so significantly, it is likely that they were losing money, too. Perhaps they were locked into a lease and figured that as long as they were forced to lease a space in the mall, they might as well use it.

So who's right: the firm that shut down because it was losing money or the firm that chose to stay open because it had to make monthly payments on its lease anyway? Ironically, both rationales are flawed. The firm that closed because it was losing money is guilty of looking at its bottom line rather than the opportunity cost of shutting down. Indeed, the business was losing money, and that wasn't likely to change with the new mall in town, but some of the expenses listed on its income statements, such as the lease payments, are fixed and would be paid whether it remained open or not. Therefore, if the firm rationalized shutting down because it was losing money, it was overestimating the opportunity cost of remaining open.

Does that mean that the firm that stayed open for business made the right decision? Not necessarily. To understand why, let's alter the scenario. Suppose you take a job in St. Louis that pays $80,000 and sign a year's lease at an apartment for $1,000/month. Three months into the lease, you get a job offer in Charlotte that promises an annual salary of $750,000. Clearly, you can't continue to live in your St. Louis apartment if you took the job in Charlotte. Would you refuse the offer because you're stuck with the lease in St. Louis? Hardly. The opportunity cost of staying in St. Louis far exceeds the benefit. A better decision would be to take the job in Charlotte and use a portion of your new salary to pay off the St. Louis lease. The same is true for the store that's saddled with a lease. "We have to pay for the lease anyway; therefore, we might as well stay open" is a poor rationale for remaining open for business. What is the opportunity cost of staying open? The firm may find that it loses less money by shutting down.

To make the right decision, the business needs to consider the available alternatives (aka the *opportunity set*) and identify the opportunity cost associated with each alternative. Let's create a hypothetical income statement

Table 1.1. Income Statements Before and After the New Mall Opens

Income statement (One month before the new mall opened)			Income statement (Four months after the new mall opened)		
Revenues:		$223,786	Revenues:		$75,670
Cost of sales:		$129,796	Cost of sales:		$43,889
Gross margin:		$93,990	Gross margin:		$31,781
Sales and marketing expenses:			Sales and marketing expenses:		
Ads:	$6,512		Ads:	$8,515	
Mailing:	$3,445	$9,957	Mailing:	$3,750	$12,265
General and administrative expenses:			General and administrative expenses:		
Payroll:	$21,530		Payroll:	$20,120	
Depreciation:	$2,250		Depreciation:	$2,250	
Rent:			Rent:		
Fixed:	$5,000		Fixed:	$5,000	
Percentage:	$2,238		Percentage:	$0	
Insurance:	$1,200	$32,218	Insurance:	$1,200	$28,570
Profit before interest and taxes:		$51,815	Profit before interest and taxes:		($9,054)
Interest:		$1,200	Interest:		$1,200
Profit before tax:		$50,615	Profit before tax:		($10,254)
Tax:		$17,715	Tax:		$0
Profit after tax:		$32,900	Profit after tax:		($10,254)

for a shoe store at the older mall. Table 1.1 shows the store's income statement one month before the new mall opened and four months after it opened. If we jump to the bottom line, we can see the store earned an after-tax profit of $32,900 before the opening of the new mall, but lost $10,254 four months after the new mall opened for business.

At first glance, it seems obvious that the store should close its doors. It's already losing more than $10,000/month, and with the new mall responsible for the drop-off in business, it is not a situation that is likely to reverse itself.

But this is why the economic approach to decision making is so important. Income statements report the sum of all revenues and expenses incurred between two discrete points in time. The key is to look for changes in revenues and expenses that are tied to specific decisions.

The shoe store was thriving before the new mall was built, but is likely to continue to lose money in its present location. What are its alternatives? Let's begin with the obvious one: shutting down. What is the opportunity cost of shutting down? The income statement shows a revenue stream of nearly $76,000/month. If the store shuts down, will it lose $76,000/month? Not necessarily. If the store is part of a chain, it may be able to transfer its inventory to another retail outlet where the shoes could be sold at a higher price. If so, the foregone revenue from shutting down may be less than $76,000/month.

For the sake of simplicity, let's assume that this is not the case: that the shoe store is a sole proprietorship. If so, shutting down the store will cause monthly revenues to fall by roughly $76,000/month.[3]

Next, we need to determine the costs relevant to shutting down. The first cost item in the income statement is the cost of sales. This reflects the cost of the inventory that was sold. Clearly, if the store closes its doors, the firm will no longer have to stock inventory. Under our assumption of a sole proprietorship, the cost of sales represents a decrease in costs associated with closing the store.

Let's proceed to the next line item, which is composed of sales and marketing expenses. Clearly, if the firm shuts down, it will no longer purchase ads or mail promotional materials to potential customers. However, the decreased cost may exceed the $12,265 that appears in Table 1.1. With the decline in foot traffic, retailers at the Indian Mall were concerned that customers were not aware that they were still in business or that they were offering their inventory on sale, so they were increasing their promotional expenditures beyond the normal level.[4]

The next items are the general and administrative expenses. The income statement reveals a monthly payroll of $20,120. Clearly, this expenditure will be eliminated if the store closes; hence, it is relevant to this decision. Will the payroll decline by $20,120? Not necessarily. The payroll reflects the number of persons employed to handle the flow of customers. With demand on the decline, the firm may not have to staff as many employees, particularly during the leanest hours.

What about depreciation? Although the income statements list a monthly depreciation expenditure of $2,250, this is not a cash flow. Rather, depreciation is an accounting procedure to allow the cost of assets to be spread out over their useful life. Because the assets have already been purchased, they are not part of the opportunity cost of shutting down.

The shoe store's rent consists of two components: fixed rent and percentage rent. Fixed rent refers to a monthly payment that must be made to lease the space regardless of the volume of sales. By contrast, percentage rent frequently appears in lease agreements for retailers in shopping malls. Typically, a *breakpoint* level of sales is negotiated between the mall and the retailer. If sales exceed the breakpoint, additional rent (usually a small percentage of the additional sales revenues) must be paid to the mall. If sales fail to reach the breakpoint level, no additional rent is paid beyond the fixed amount.

The income statements in Table 1.1 reveal a monthly fixed payment of $5,000. Because the retailer must honor the lease regardless of whether it remains open or shuts down, the fixed rent is not relevant to the decision. However, lease agreements often contain clauses that call for fixed payments if the lease is terminated prematurely. These are frequently much less than the remaining monthly fixed payment for the duration of the lease. As an example, suppose the retailer has eight months remaining on the lease (or a total of $40,000 in fixed lease payments), but can get out of the lease if the retailer pays $10,000. In this case, the net change in lease payments is relevant to the decision. By closing down, the store reduces its fixed rent by $30,000. One should note, however, that for each month the store remains open, the reduction in fixed lease payments falls by $5,000.

The percentage rent is potentially relevant to this decision because it is tied to sales. No percentage rent is paid if the retailer ceases to do business. However, because the rent is paid only for sales beyond the prenegotiated breakpoint level, the income statement suggests that the firm's sales are currently below the breakpoint. Assuming this is a permanent state of affairs, shutting down will not result in any decrease in percentage rent.

Although insurance may be relevant to the shut-down decision, it is perhaps not for the immediate short term. The firm may have a contractual arrangement that may be terminated relatively quickly. Until the retailer is in a position to terminate its policy, insurance is not relevant.

Interest payments are expenses for debts already accumulated. Because they reflect past decisions, they are not relevant to the shut-down decision. Taxes are clearly a relevant cost because the shoe store's profits will no longer be taxed if it closes.

Table 1.2. Changes in Revenues and Costs from Closing the Store

Decision: Close the shoe store		
Decrease in revenues:		($75,670)
Decrease in costs:		
Cost of sales:	$43,889	
Ads:	$8,515	
Mailings:	$3,750	
Payroll:	$20,120	$76,274

So what's the final verdict? To begin with, we have to assess whether the revenues and expenses captured in the most recent income statement are an accurate reflection of the state of affairs for the remainder of the lease. Perhaps sales will continue to decline. For the sake of argument, let's assume a fairly static income statement for the remaining eight months of the lease such that the revenues and expenses relevant to the shut-down decision decline by the amounts listed on the statement. We've assumed that as a sole proprietorship, the store will lose its monthly revenues of $75,670. The cost of sales will fall by $43,889/month. The $12,265 in promotional expenses will also be eliminated if the store ceases to exist. Similarly, the firm will not have to incur its monthly payroll expense of $20,120. Assume the insurance expense is fixed.

According to the figures (summarized in Table 1.2), shutting down will save the store $76,274/month in operating expenses while sacrificing $75,670/month in revenues. If these figures were ironclad, the firm would save $604/month by closing. But recall that these numbers may require some tweaking. This is why decision makers need to think beyond historical costs when evaluating opportunity cost. The recorded expenses make for a reasonable starting point, but may not accurately capture the opportunity of shutting down. Promotional expenses are equal to 16% of revenues. Can the store reduce its advertising without cutting appreciably into its revenue stream? The payroll is very nearly the same as it was before the decline in sales. Is the store staffing too many employees relative to the current level of demand? Because demand has been falling, should the store consider cutting the price of its shoes to increase revenues?

Suppose the owner infers that he can reduce operating expenditures such that the store can make a small profit over the remainder of the lease. Should the store remain open? Not necessarily. Recall that the opportunity cost of shutting down is not restricted to accounting expenses. As an alternative to keeping the store open, the owner could invest the monthly operating expenses and earn interest and dividends. He could move the store to another location or get into another business entirely. The foregone earnings from remaining at the Indian Mall comprise the opportunity cost of remaining at the mall and will factor into his decision.

So what does economics have to offer to the business manager? Quite a lot, obviously. Whereas balance sheets summarize a stock of assets and liabilities, and the income statements report the flow of revenues and expenses between two points in time, economics focuses on evaluating opportunity costs. As the mall example illustrates, microeconomic theory contains many useful insights that can help a business manager make more effective decisions.

Summary

- Economics is a social science that studies how people deal with constraints in pursuit of a goal.
- When people make decisions, they forego alternatives. Opportunity cost is the highest valued alternative gone. It plays a role in every decision we make.
- Because decisions are inherently future acts, the opportunity cost of a decision is always forward thinking.
- Accounting costs reflect the historical cost of past decisions. They should not be equated with opportunity costs. However, they make for a convenient benchmark upon which opportunity costs may be assessed.

CHAPTER 2

What Matters and What Doesn't: Relevant Revenues and Costs

The primary goal of a firm is to maximize profits. This implies, of course, that each decision a manager makes is consistent with that goal. Although managers are expected to rely on internally produced reports to help them make decisions, most of the information that appears on these statements is period based rather than decision based. A balance sheet shows the sum total of a firm's assets and liabilities at a given point in time. If the firm sold off all of its assets at book value and used the proceeds to pay its liabilities, what remains is owner's equity, which is the amount that is owed to shareholders. An income statement is the difference between revenues and expenses between two points in time.

A myriad of useful pieces of information can be gleaned from these statements: the current ratio, inventory ratio, and liabilities ratio may be determined from balance sheets. Net sales to inventory and net profits to net sales are obtained from income statements. But as useful as this information can be to managers, the critical element is that the balance sheet and income statement represent the collective results of previous decisions. The balance sheet indicates where the firm stands as a result of all past decisions. The income statement reports the revenues received and expenses incurred between two distinct dates. Some of the revenues may flow from decisions made in previous periods. Some of the expenses that are incurred may not generate revenue until a future period. There is nothing in the statement that reports the results of a specific decision.

But managers need to know how to make profitable decisions. Economists and accountants assert that managers should compare the *relevant revenues* and *relevant costs* associated with a decision.[1] Relevant revenues refer to any revenues that will change if the decision is implemented. Any revenue that will remain unchanged is irrelevant and should be disregarded in evaluating a course of action. Relevant costs refer to any costs that will change if the decision is implemented. Any costs that remain unchanged should not be factored into the firm's decision.

Let's use several contrasting examples. A local group decides to hold a fundraiser by selling boxes of chocolate chip cookies. Each box costs the group $3. Historically, it charged a price of $10/box and sold 300 boxes. This year, the group is considering lowering its price to sell more boxes. It believes it could sell 400 boxes at a price of $8/box. The decision is whether to lower the price to $8 to sell more boxes. If the decision is implemented, revenues will rise from $3,000 to $3,200, or by $200. The $200 increase in revenue is the relevant revenue. The relevant revenue, however, is not simply the revenues generated by the additional 100 boxes. If that were true, revenues would rise by $8 × 100 boxes, or $800. Instead, the relevant revenues incorporate the fact that the 300 boxes that could have been sold for $10 will also be sold for $8. In other words, to sell the additional 100 boxes for $800, the group sacrificed $600 on the first 300 boxes. Hence, the decision caused the group's revenue to rise by $800 – $600, or $200.

The relevant cost in this example is the change in the group's cost if the decision to lower the price is implemented. Because each box costs the group $3, if it lowers the price to $8, it will sell 100 additional boxes at a cost of $3, causing costs to rise by $300.

If we compare the relevant revenues with the relevant costs, we can see that the group should not lower its price. If it does, its revenues will rise by $200, whereas its cost will increase by $300. It will be $100 worse off by lowering its price.

This can also be seen by examining total revenues and costs. At a price of $10, the group's revenue is $10 × 300, or $3,000 and its costs are $3 × 300, or $900, leaving a profit of $2,100. If it charges $8, its revenues will be $3,200 ($8 × 400) and its costs will be equal to $1,200 ($3 × 400), for a profit of $2,000. By lowering its price, its profits decline by $100. This is summarized in Table 2.1.

Table 2.1. *Relevant Revenue and Relevant Cost: Example 1*

Decision: Lower the Price from $10 to $8				
	Total revenue	Relevant revenue	Total cost	Relevant cost
Decision not implemented	$3,000		$900	
Decision implemented	$3,200		$1,200	
		$200		$300

Table 2.2. *Relevant Revenue and Relevant Cost: Example 2*

Decision: Lower the Price from $10 to $8 for senior citizens only				
	Total revenue	Relevant revenue	Total cost	Relevant cost
Decision not implemented	$3,000		$900	
Decision implemented	$3,800		$1,200	
		$800		$300

Although this is a relatively simple example, one might see how poor decisions might have been made without relying on relevant revenues and costs. For example, each box costs the group $3 and would be priced at $8. At face value, one might be deluded into thinking that the group's profits would rise by $500 ($5 profit/box times 100 additional boxes) if the price were lowered. In fact, the decision would have caused the group's profits to fall because the first 300 boxes would also be sold at the lower price. Let's expand on the previous example to show how relevant revenues and costs can become complicated. Suppose the group is considering offering a senior citizen discount on boxes. The seniors will pay $8, whereas everyone else will pay $10. Consistent with the previous example, 300 boxes can be sold for $10 and 100 additional boxes can be sold for $8. In this case, the relevant revenue is $800. The group will collect an additional $800 from the 100 boxes, and none of that will be offset by lower prices charged on the first 300 boxes. Because the relevant costs associated with the decision to set a separate price for senior citizens is $300, the group's net income will rise by $500. This is illustrated in Table 2.2.

Table 2.3. Relevant Revenue and Relevant Cost: Example 3

Decision: Lower the Price from $10 to $8				
	Total revenue	Relevant revenue	Total cost	Relevant cost
Decision not implemented	$3,000		$1,200	
Decision implemented	$3,800		$1,600	
		$800		$400

Let's go back to the single price example, but make adjustments on costs. A local supermarket is allowing the group to sell its cookies outside the store, but requires the group to pay $1 for each box it sells. The group has already sold 300 boxes. It is going to purchase 100 more boxes, but is considering lowering its price from $10 to $8 to sell them. Because 300 boxes have already been sold, the relevant revenue is $8 × 100, or $800. What is the relevant cost? The $300 paid to the supermarket for the first 300 boxes is a *sunk cost*. A sunk cost is a cost that will not change if the decision is implemented. Sunk costs are never relevant to any decision. In this case, the relevant costs are equal to $400: each of the 100 additional boxes cost the group $3. In addition, the group must pay the supermarket $100 for the additional unit sales ($1/box multiplied by 100 boxes). If the group lowers its price, its net income will increase by $400. This result is seen in Table 2.3.

Let's make another change to the scenario. This time, the group pre-orders 400 boxes in the belief it can sell them for $10 each. Once ordered, the boxes cannot be returned for a refund. Unit sales are slower than anticipated. The group sees that it will sell no more than 300 boxes unless it lowers its price to $8. Should the price be lowered? Our assumption is that 300 boxes have already been sold for $10. The relevant revenues will be equal to the additional revenues generated by the extra 100 boxes, or $800. What are the relevant costs? Under the arrangement with the supermarket, the group will have to pay $1/box or an additional $100. What about the cost of the boxes? Indeed, the group paid $3 for each of the 400 boxes. However, because the boxes cannot be returned for a refund, this cost is now a sunk cost and not relevant to the decision. Thus, the relevant cost is

Table 2.4. Relevant Revenue and Relevant Cost: Example 4

Decision: Lower the Price from $10 to $8				
	Total revenue	Relevant revenue	Total cost	Relevant cost
Decision not implemented	$3,000		$1,500	
Decision implemented	$3,800		$1,600	
		$800		$100

$100. If the group lowers its price to $8 to sell the additional 100 boxes, its net income will increase by $700.

If this seems confusing, let's examine the overall ramifications. If the price remains at $10, the group will sell 300 boxes and generate $3,000 in revenue. The costs will consist of the $1,200 paid for the boxes ($3 × 400) and also $300 paid to the supermarket ($1 × 300) for a total of $1,500. The fundraiser will generate net income equal to $1,500. Suppose the group lowers its price to $8 to sell the additional 100 boxes (keep in mind that 300 boxes have already been sold for $10), its revenues will total $3,800. The group's costs will equal $1,600 ($4 × 400). Net income will rise to $2,200, an increase of $700, as shown in Table 2.4.

Let's take this last example and give it another twist. The fundraiser is nearly over. The group realizes it ordered too many boxes of cookies and is considering lowering its price to sell them. What is the lowest price the group should charge? At first glance, one might assume the breakeven price is $4. After all, the group paid $3/box and each additional box sold requires a $1 payment to the supermarket. So the group will lose money on each box sold for less than $4. But this is where the importance of sunk costs comes into play. The group prepaid for 400 boxes and cannot return any unsold boxes for a full or partial refund. Although the decision to order 400 boxes may be one they regret, the cost of the 400 boxes is not relevant to any subsequent decision. The only additional cost the group will bear by selling more boxes is the $1/box paid to the supermarket. This means the group should be willing to lower its price to no less than $1.

How could this be? Doesn't this imply the group will be selling the additional boxes below cost? Table 2.5 illustrates the results. The first

Table 2.5. Relevant Revenue and Relevant Cost: Example 5

Decision: Lower the Price from $10 to $1.50 for the remaining 100 boxes				
	Total revenue	Relevant revenue	Total cost	Relevant cost
Decision not implemented	$3,000		$1,500	
Decision implemented	$3,150		$1,600	
		$150		$100

300 boxes were sold for $10/box. Because the group did not want to leave with unsold boxes, it drops the price to $1.50/box for the remaining 100 boxes. Because the relevant cost of the last 100 boxes is $1/box, the group increases its net income by $50 when it lowered the price of the remaining boxes to $1.50.

It is critical to note that relevant cost cannot be determined a priori. Rather, relevance is defined by the decision. In the last example, we decided that the $3/box cost of the cookies was a sunk cost and, therefore, irrelevant. This is why it made sense for the group to lower the price to $1.50 to dump the remaining boxes. Suppose the group had only ordered 300 boxes. Once the fundraiser got under way, the group believed it could sell more. Assume the supplier is local, allowing the group to purchase additional cookies to sell. If the group were to consider purchasing 100 additional boxes, what is the lowest price it should consider charging? Note that in this case, the $3/box cost is no longer sunk. It represents a relevant cost associated with selling 100 more boxes. Coupled with the $1/box payment to the supermarket, if the group wishes to purchase 100 more boxes, it must be willing to charge a price no less than $4 to make the effort worthwhile. This is shown in Table 2.6. Let's assume the additional boxes are sold for $5 each. The increase in profit is simply the difference between the relevant revenues ($5/box multiplied by 100 additional boxes) and the relevant costs ($4/box multiplied by 100 additional boxes). The critical notion is that a cost is sunk only if it cannot be changed by the decision under consideration; if the decision may cause it to change, the cost is relevant. As this example illustrates, a cost that was not considered relevant to one decision may be relevant to another.

Table 2.6. Relevant Revenue and Relevant Cost: Example 6

Decision: Purchase 100 additional boxes				
	Total revenue	Relevant revenue	Total cost	Relevant cost
Decision not implemented	$3,000		$1,200	
Decision implemented	$3,500		$1,600	
		$500		$400

Table 2.7. Relevant Revenue and Relevant Cost: Example 7

Decision: Sell remaining 100 boxes for $.01/box				
	Total revenue	Relevant revenue	Total cost	Relevant cost
Decision not implemented	$3,000		$1,600	
Decision implemented	$3,001		$1,600	
		$1		$0

Let's make another change in the analysis. We will return to the assumption that 400 boxes were preordered and cannot be returned for a partial refund. Moreover, rather than pay $1/box, the supermarket charges a flat fee of $400. If the group wishes to lower the price to dump the remaining 100 boxes, what is the lowest price it should entertain?

Although the flat fee ($400) divided by 400 boxes is still $1, the break-even price is no longer $1. In this instance, the entire fee becomes a sunk cost. The group will pay $400 to the supermarket regardless of whether it sells 300 boxes or 400 boxes. The $3 cost per box is also a sunk cost because unsold boxes cannot be returned for a refund. This implies that the group could lower the price to $0 without being worse off. We can illustrate this in Table 2.7. We will assume the first 300 boxes were sold for $10/box and the remaining 100 boxes were sold for 1¢ each.

As the table indicates, if the firm does not lower its price for the remaining boxes, it will generate $3,000 in revenue. Selling the remaining 100 boxes at $.01/box generates an additional $1 in revenue. Four hundred boxes were prepaid at a cost of $3/box. In addition, the group paid a flat fee of $400 for the right to hold its fundraiser on supermarket

Table 2.8. Unit Cost Estimates for Fundraiser

Expense category	Amount
Boxes of cookies	$900
Supermarket fee	$200
Promotional and other	$100
Total	$1,200
Cost/box	$1,200/300 = $4

property. This implies the group bears costs of $1,600 regardless of how many boxes it sells. Lowering the price on the remaining 100 boxes does not force the group to incur any additional costs, so the relevant cost associated with the decision is $0. Thus, the decision adds $1 to the net income of the group.

Let's try one more example that will bring us in focus with the theme of this book. The group has a treasurer who collects past expenses. The group will rely on her cost data to set prices. She gathered data from the previous year's fundraiser. In that year, the group paid a flat fee of $200 to hold its fundraiser. The cost of each box was $3. Promotional and other miscellaneous expenses totaled $100. As the previous year's fundraiser resulted in 300 boxes being sold, she reports the cost/box to be $4, as shown in Table 2.8. Based on her estimates, she advises selling the boxes for a price no less than $4/box.

Is the treasurer correct in her analysis? What is the relevant cost associated with selling one box of cookies? If none of these expenses have yet been incurred, then one might surmise that they are all relevant costs. That's not quite correct. They are all relevant costs if the decision is whether to hold a fundraiser at all. In that case, the group's relevant cost would be $300 + $3Q, where Q is the number of boxes sold. Because the revenue generated from sales is $P \times Q$, the lowest feasible price for holding the fundraiser would be determined by setting total revenue equal to total cost and solving for the price. In other words,

$$\text{Total Revenue} = \text{Total Cost}$$
$$P \times Q = \$300 + \$3Q$$
$$P = (\$300 + 3Q)/Q$$

Keep in mind that this equation does not determine what price the group should charge. Rather, it indicates the minimum price the group should charge if it wants to sell a given quantity of boxes and break even. For example, if the group wants to sell 100 boxes, it would need to be able to charge ($300 + $3 × 100)/100, or $6 to break even. If the group wishes to sell 400 boxes, it would have to sell the boxes at a price of at least ($300 + $3 × 400)/400, or $3.75 to break even.

It is important to note that the equation does not imply that the group can sell the desired quantity of boxes at that price; rather, it only indicates the minimum price necessary to generate enough money to cover its costs. Managers need to understand that breakeven pricing is not an indication of consumer demand. In this circumstance, the group would need to determine if selling 100 boxes at $6/box or 400 boxes at $3.75/box was feasible.

This can be illustrated with an exaggerated example. Suppose the group wanted to sell only two boxes. The minimum price necessary to hold the fundraiser would be ($300 + $3 × 2)/2, or $153. Clearly, the group cannot expect to be able to charge $153 for a box of cookies and expect to sell them.[2]

The group decides to go ahead with the fundraiser. At this point, the supermarket fee and the promotional expenses become sunk costs.[3] They are no longer relevant to the pricing of a box of cookies. From this point forward, only the $3 cost/box is relevant to pricing decisions.

If the reader is still unconvinced, let's make a change in the analysis. Suppose last year's fundraiser took place in a pounding rain with 35 MPH winds. As a result, the group only sold ten boxes. If so, the average cost per box would be $33, as shown in Table 2.9.

Would you follow the treasurer's advice to charge no less than $33/box for this year's fundraiser? If we eliminate the irrelevant costs, we see that the only cost relevant to price setting is the $3 cost of each box.

There is another element in the analysis worth noting. The supermarket charged a flat fee of $200 for the previous year's fundraiser, but is raising the fee to $400 this year. Is this cost relevant to the decision to hold the fundraiser? Of course, it is. The flat fee for last year's fundraiser has no bearing on this year's fundraiser. Historical costs have no bearing on decisions. Only expected future costs matter.

Table 2.9. Unit Cost Estimates for Fundraiser (10 boxes sold)

Expense category	Amount
Boxes of cookies	$30
Supermarket fee	$200
Promotional and other	$100
Total	$330
Cost/box	$330/10 = $33

This has a great deal of importance to managers. Unit cost estimates are invariably based on historical costs. But decisions take place in the future. Only if past cost patterns continue will the unit cost data correctly reflect expected future costs.

We can examine balance sheets from the same perspective. In theory, the balance sheet reveals how much money will be left over if the firm sells off all of its assets and uses the funds to pay its liabilities. But is this necessarily the case? Most accountants report their assets in terms of their book value, not their current market value. They also rely on a depreciation method to infer the current depreciated value of the asset. Accountants generally acknowledge that many assets wear out over time, diminishing their salvage value, but the rate at which they wear out is unknown. Consequently, accountants depreciate their assets according to one of many conventionally accepted methods. But the depreciation expense is only an estimate of the rate at which the assets wear out. Thus, the value of the asset, calculated as its book value less accumulate depreciation may be an inaccurate reflection of its true salvage value.

Many accountants have taken to **mark-to-market** accounting to better reflect the assets' (or liabilities') current value. Unfortunately, because the current market value of an asset could not always be objectively determined, this technique opened up the potential for accounting fraud, such as that revealed in the Enron scandal. In its original business model, the Enron relied on actual expenses incurred and actual revenues received. When mark-to-market accounting was implemented in its trading business, the present value of inflows from long-term contracts was recognized as revenues and the present value of expected future costs was expensed.

Of course, one might expect the present value of future inflows to be rather speculative. As an example, Enron signed a 20-year deal with Blockbuster to provide video on demand to various markets. Pilot projects were set up in Portland, Seattle, and Salt Lake City. Based on the results of the pilot projects, Enron logged profits of $110 million even though there were questions about its viability and market demand.[4]

Our examples showed that determining relevant revenues and costs requires a bit of thought. Let's break it down into its pieces. First, we need to distinguish between *fixed costs* and *variable costs*. Fixed costs are expenses that do not vary with output. Examples include the group's promotional expenses or the flat fee that it might have paid the supermarket. We can also break fixed costs into two subcategories. *Avoidable fixed costs* are fixed expenses that are incurred only if the decision is implemented. *Unavoidable fixed costs* are fixed costs that remain unchanged if the decision is implemented. Unavoidable fixed costs are, by definition, sunk costs, and are not relevant to decisions.

It is important to note that categorizing an expense as avoidable or unavoidable cannot be done a priori. Rather, the decision defines the expense. For example, if the group is trying to determine whether to hold the fundraiser, the promotional expenses are avoidable fixed costs. If the fundraiser is held, the group will incur this expense; if the fundraiser is not held, there are no promotional expenses. Avoidable fixed costs are relevant costs. Once the group goes ahead with the fundraiser, the promotional expense becomes an unavoidable fixed cost. The group has committed to the expense and cannot recover it. Therefore, it is not relevant to any subsequent decision.[5]

Variable costs are expenses that vary with production. Each box of cookies cost the group $3. Consequently, the more boxes they wanted to sell, the higher the cost. Because most decisions involve changes in production, variable costs are usually relevant costs.

Categorizing avoidable fixed costs, unavoidable fixed costs, and variable costs allows us to understand relevant costs. Avoidable fixed costs are always relevant costs because they change if the decision is implemented. Unavoidable fixed costs are never relevant costs because they are sunk. Variable costs are relevant costs in most circumstances because the majority of decisions entail changes in production or the unit costs associated with production. An example of where variable costs are not relevant is when the firm wants to shift production from one facility to another because the lease offers more favorable terms. If unit costs are not going to be different and the firm does not expect to change production levels, the difference in the terms of the lease is the only relevant cost.

If we apply these definitions to the fundraiser examples, we can see why some costs were categorized as relevant and why others were not. When deciding whether to lower the price from $10 to $8, the $3/box cost was relevant because it was a variable that would rise with each additional box sold. When 400 boxes were prepurchased, the expenditure became an unavoidable fixed cost because the group had expended $1,200, and that cost would not change regardless of how many boxes went unsold. Similarly, the $1/box payment was a variable cost that would be relevant to the pricing decision. The flat fee to be paid to the supermarket would be an avoidable fixed cost if the group is considering whether to hold a fundraiser, but it would be an unavoidable fixed cost when it comes to pricing decisions.

Summary

- Decisions should be based on relevant revenues and relevant costs. Relevant revenues are revenues that will change if the decision is implemented. Relevant costs are costs that will change if the decision is implemented.
- Fixed costs are costs that do not vary with production. Unavoidable fixed costs are fixed costs that will not change if the decision is implemented. Unavoidable fixed costs are sunk costs and are not relevant to decisions. Avoidable fixed costs are fixed costs that will change if the decision is implemented. Avoidable fixed costs are relevant costs.
- Variable costs are costs that vary with production. Because most decisions affect production, variable costs are usually relevant costs.

CHAPTER 3

Determining Relevant Revenues: Understanding the Buyer

The Law of Demand

1. Individual Demand

The previous chapter was devoted to a discussion of relevant revenues and costs. To maximize profits, firms must determine the changes in revenues (relevant revenues) associated with a given decision. Consumer choice theory can be very useful in helping managers to determine relevant revenues.

To understand consumer behavior, we have to recognize the role of opportunity cost. Consumers don't have to buy from your firm. From their point of view, the price of your good represents opportunity cost: if they pay $100 to buy your good, they cannot spend it on other goods and services they may value. Thus, the consumer will weigh your good against those produced by competing firms. Even if no viable competitors exist for your product, the consumer may choose to dedicate the $100 to unrelated goods the individual values.

Consumer choice theory allows us to understand how buyers make choices in the face of opportunity cost. Suppose you are going to the ballgame and expect to buy concessions while you're there. At a break in the game, you decide to buy a beer. A 16-ounce beer costs $5. Five dollars certainly won't break you, and in fact, you have $20 in your wallet. To you, the issue is not whether you like or could afford a beer, but whether the beer gives you as much satisfaction as anything else you could buy with $5. Hence, you weigh the satisfaction from drinking a beer against the satisfaction you could obtain from spending the $5 on other goods and services. Your decision may or may not hinge on the price of other concessions. You could decide not to buy any concessions at the game and to spend your money after the game on whatever you choose. You may not even spend the money the same day. The key is that you evaluate buying the beer against all other alternatives.

This is the essence of consumer choice theory: to derive a theory that describes a consumer's behavior. Let's continue with our ballgame example. You visit the concessions stand. You must decide between buying a hot dog and buying a beer. Suppose hot dogs also cost $5. Because both goods have the same price, you will purchase the good that gives you the most satisfaction. Economists use the word *utility* to refer to satisfaction. *Marginal utility* refers to the satisfaction the individual obtains from one more unit of the good. If you decide to buy the hot dog, we can infer that the marginal utility of the first hot dog (MU_{HD}^1) gives you more satisfaction than the first beer (MU_B^1). Later in the game, you return to the concessions stand. This time, you buy the beer. It must be true that the marginal utility from the first beer (MU_B^1) (i.e. additional satisfaction) exceeds the marginal utility from the second hot dog (MU_{HD}^2).

Your buying habits establish the framework that describes consumer demand. You preferred the first hot dog to the first beer, but you would rather have your first beer than your second hot dog. Let's review your preferences:

1. $MU_{HD}^1 > MU_B^1$ (the first hot dog is preferred to the first beer)
2. $MU_B^1 > MU_{HD}^2$ (the first beer is preferred to the second hot dog)
   If the first hot dog is preferred to the first beer, but the first beer is preferred to the second hot dog, it also follows that the first hot dog is preferred to the second hot dog, or:
3. $MU_{HD}^1 > MU_{HD}^2$ (the first hot dog is preferred to the second hot dog)

Economists refer to this as the *law of diminishing marginal utility*. It suggests that the additional satisfaction derived from each additional unit diminishes as more units are consumed. If this were not true, you would go to the game and spend all of your money on hot dogs. Because consumers spread their money around to buy a wide array of products, we can infer the law of diminishing marginal utility plays a role in virtually all purchase decisions.

If the law of diminishing marginal utility states that each unit provides the buyer with less additional satisfaction, it must also be true that the buyer is willing to spend less on each additional unit. Thus, if the buyer is willing to spend up to $3.75 for the first hot dog, he will be willing to spend less than $3.75 for the second hot dog, and even less for the third hot dog. Suppose the consumer is willing to spend up to $2.50 for the second hot dog, and $1.25 for the third hot dog. This allows us to derive the *law of demand*. If the price of hot dogs is $3.75, the buyer would only be willing to buy one because the other hot dogs do not provide sufficient satisfaction to justify the opportunity cost. If the price of hot dogs fell to $2.50, he would be willing to buy two hot dogs. The second hot dog now justifies the expenditure, but the third one does not. *The law of demand states that as the price of a good rises, the quantity demanded decreases, and vice versa.*

The individual's demand for hot dogs appears in Table 3.1 and is expressed graphically in Figure 3.1.

Table 3.1. Individual Demand
Schedule

Quantity	Willing to spend
1	$3.75
2	$2.50
3	$1.25

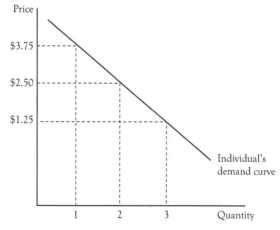

Figure 3.1. Individual demand curve.

Table 3.2. Demand Schedule for the Firm

| Price | Quantity demanded by | | | |
	Amber	Bruce	Casey	Total demand
$3.75	0	1	1	2
$2.50	1	2	1	4
$1.25	2	2	2	6

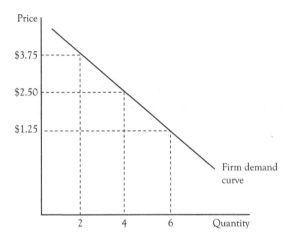

Figure 3.2. Firm demand curve.

2. Demand Faced by the Firm

The **demand** for the good produced by the firm indicates the quantities of a firm's good or services that buyers are willing and able to buy at each price. It is simply the sum of the quantities demanded by each individual consumer. An example appears in Table 3.2, with the corresponding firm demand curve illustrated in Figure 3.2.

The Law of Demand and Marginal Revenue

The law of demand asserts that as the price of the good rises, the quantity demanded by consumers falls. Conversely, the law also states that the more units the firm wishes to sell, the lower the price it must charge.

Netflix encountered the law of demand when it developed Qwikster. Netflix established its position in the DVD rental market with its rent-by-mail system. As downloading became increasingly popular, the firm sought to segment its market. Subscribers could continue to order DVDs by mail. Others could subscribe to its cheaper downloading service, which it named Qwikster. But Netflix subscribers could already download in addition to order by mail, so what Netflix saw as a means to segment its market, its subscribers saw as a 60% increase in the price of subscriptions. In response to falling subscriptions and widespread subscriber outrage, Qwikster was abandoned.[1]

An important component to determining relevant revenue is marginal revenue. Marginal revenue is the additional revenue generated by an additional unit of output. Clearly, when determining whether to increase production, the firm wants to know how much additional revenue will be generated. Such decisions cannot be made in a vacuum. The firm cannot assume that any and all of its additional production can be sold at the existing price. Instead, the quantity it sells is going to be influenced by the law of demand.

At first glance, one might assume that the marginal revenue generated by a unit of output is equal to its price. But this is not the case. To illustrate, examine the information in Table 3.2. If the firm charges $2.50, it can sell four hot dogs. If it lowers the price to $1.25, it can sell six hot dogs. Is the marginal revenue from the two additional hot dogs $2.50 ($1.25 x two additional hot dogs)?

Let's examine this decision closely. According to Table 3.2, it can sell four hot dogs at a price of $2.50. This would generate revenues totaling $10. If it lowers the price to $1.25, the firm could sell six hot dogs. Note that the firm's revenue under this price would fall to $7.50. Thus, increasing unit sales from four hot dogs to six hot dogs didn't cause the firm's revenue to rise by $2.50; in fact, it caused revenue to *fall* by $2.50. Why?

If we break the decision down into two parts, we can see what happened. On the one hand, the firm sold two additional hot dogs at a price of $1.25 each. Economists refer to the $2.50 generated by the two hot dogs as the **output effect**. But this is only half the story. When the firm decided to sell six hot dogs, it lowered the price from $2.50 to $1.25 on all six hot dogs, not just the last two. Therefore, in addition to selling two additional hot dogs for $1.25 each, the firm lowered the price on the first four hot dogs from $2.50 to $1.25. In other words, the firm has to forego $5 ($1.25 on each of the first four hot dogs) in order to sell six hot dogs. The $1.25 price reduction on the first four hot dogs is called the

price effect. The marginal revenue is the sum of the output and price effects. In this case, by increasing unit sales from four hot dogs to six hot dogs, the firm's revenue changed by the sum of the output ($2.50) and price effects (–$5), or a decrease of $2.50.

To develop the relationship between firm demand and marginal revenue, examine Table 3.3. If the firm wishes to sell one unit, it can charge a price as high as $10, which yields $10 in total revenue. The marginal revenue from the first unit, therefore, is $10. If the firm wants to sell two units, it must drop the price from $10 to $9. This will cause revenues to rise from $10 to $18, an increase of $8. If the firm wants to sell three units, it must lower its price from $9 to $8. This will cause revenues to increase by $6 (from $18 to $24).

Note that aside from the first unit, the marginal revenue from each unit is less than the price. For example, the second unit can be sold for $9, but it only increases revenues by $8. The third unit can be sold for $8, but it will only cause revenues to rise by $6. Marginal revenue is less than the price because of the price effect; the extra revenue generated by the additional unit is at least partially offset by the lower price on the other units. This can be

Table 3.3. Firm Demand and Marginal Revenue

Price	Firm demand	Total revenue	Marginal revenue
$10	1	$10	$10
$9	2	$18	$8
$8	3	$24	$6

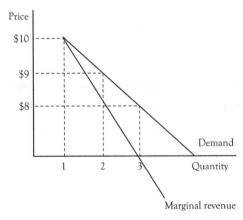

Figure 3.3. Demand curve and marginal revenue.

seen in Figure 3.3. Because marginal revenue is less than the price for all but the first unit, the marginal revenue curve lies below the demand curve.

The implications of the law of demand on marginal revenue cannot be understated. Sound decision making requires the manager to determine the relevant revenue pertaining to a decision. It is too convenient to assume that marginal revenue consists only of output effects. But the law of demand states that most production increases necessitate lowering the price. For this reason, it is imperative that firms consider potential price effects when determining relevant revenues.

Factors That Change Demand

In addition to price changes, consumers respond to changes in other factors. Suppose the price charged by a competitor rises. As a result, some of his customers may decide to buy from your firm instead, even though you have not changed your price. This is illustrated in Figure 3.4. The original demand curve is shown as D_1. At the current price of $10, 100 units are sold. After the competitor increased its price, the demand for your good increased to D_2, a shift to the right. This allows you to sell 150 units at the same price. In essence, an increase in the price of a substitute caused the demand for your good to increase.

Demand can also change if the price of a complementary good changes. An example appears in Figure 3.5. Assume the price of a bag of

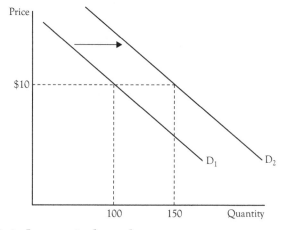

Figure 3.4. Increase in demand.

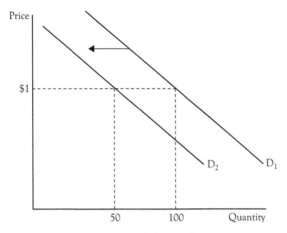

Figure 3.5. Decrease in demand for French fries.

French fries is $1 and the price of a hamburger is $1.50. At these prices, the demand for fries is characterized by D_1, and the quantity of fries demanded is 100. If the price of hamburgers rises to $2, not only will consumers buy fewer hamburgers, they will also purchase fewer bags of fries. Thus, the demand for fries decreases, shifting the demand curve to the left. At the new level of demand, 50 bags of fries are demanded.

Income changes can also affect demand. Although we generally think that increases in income will increase demand, this is not always the case. When consumer incomes rise, the demand for used cars may fall as consumers substitute into buying new cars. Economists label goods whose demand rises when incomes rise as **normal goods**. If demand decreases in response to an increase in income (such as our used car example), the good is called an **inferior good**.

Changes in consumer tastes can cause demand to increase or decrease. Some goods are seasonal in nature. The demand for snow skis rises in the winter and falls in the summer. Some goods become obsolete. As cell phones became more popular, the demand for landline phones decreased.

Changes in price expectations can affect demand. After the terrorist attacks on 9/11, consumers feared gas prices would skyrocket and rushed off to fill their tanks. The result was long gas lines and, ironically, higher gas prices.[2] The higher prices were not created by the attacks, but rather, by the panic that led everyone to try to fill their tanks on the same day.

The Price Elasticity of Demand

Another key element of demand theory that is critical to determining relevant revenue is the ***price elasticity of demand***. The law of demand asserts that as the price rises, the quantity demanded falls. The price elasticity of demand expands on the law of demand: it measures the responsiveness of the quantity demanded to price changes. Drivers inevitably grumble about rising gasoline prices. Many individuals regard driving as a necessity because they simply live too far from work, school, or other destinations to walk or ride a bike. Moreover, their cars only run on gas: they can't pump water into their tanks if the price of gas becomes too costly. As a result, when gas prices rise, consumers may cut back on their gasoline consumption a little, but not by a whole lot. But consumers are less likely to complain about the rising price of frozen yogurt. Unlike gas, frozen yogurt is unlikely to be viewed as a necessity. If the consumer thinks the price is too high, he can simply do without. Moreover, ice cream and frozen custard are reasonably close substitutes for frozen yogurt. If the price of frozen yogurt rises, the consumer can substitute into ice cream.

Let's illustrate the concept of price elasticity graphically. Figure 3.6 shows the demand curves for gasoline and frozen yogurt. Note that whereas the law of demand holds in both cases, a given increase in the price leads to a larger decrease in the quantity of frozen yogurt demanded relative to the

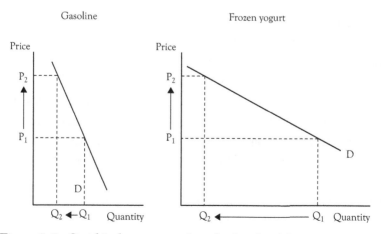

Figure 3.6. Graphical representation of price elasticity.

decline in the quantity of gasoline demanded. When the quantity demanded of a given product is relatively responsive to price changes (i.e. frozen yogurt), we say that good has a relatively *elastic* demand. When the quantity demanded of a good is not very responsive to price changes (i.e. gasoline), we say the good has a relatively *inelastic* demand.

What determines price elasticity? We have already covered two determinants. The first is whether the good is a luxury or a necessity. If a good is considered to be a luxury, the prospective buyer may choose not to buy it if the price is too high. This is why the travel industry often suffers during recessions. Families are less likely to go on a vacation if one or more of the parents are unemployed or fears losing his job. If the product is viewed as a necessity, on the other hand, the consumer may have no choice but to continue to buy the good.

Another determinant is the availability of substitutes. When the price of a good rises, they look for cheaper substitutes. When the price of frozen yogurt rises, they can substitute into ice cream, whereas the drivers cannot opt for cheaper substitutes when the price of gasoline rises.

This is why gasoline is a frequent government target for taxation. In 1980, the federal gasoline tax was 4 cents per gallon. By 1993, the tax had risen to its current level of 18.4 cents per gallon. And this is only the federal tax. Each state has its own tax, ranging from roughly ten cents per gallon to 40 cents per gallon.[3] Gasoline is a target for taxation because consumers cannot cut back significantly on their gasoline consumption when prices rise.

Another determinant of price elasticity that relates to the availability of substitutes is the definition of the market. Whereas consumers may view the demand for gasoline to be relatively inelastic, the same cannot be said for the gasoline sold at the gas station on the corner of First and Main. Consumers may have few alternatives when the price of gasoline rises, but they can easily substitute away from the gasoline sold at a specific station by purchasing gas from a competing station. Thus, whereas the demand for gasoline may be inelastic, the demand for gas sold by a specific retailer is highly elastic.

Another determinant of price elasticity is the price of the good as a percentage of the consumer's budget. The National Association for Convenience Stores reported an average gross margin of nearly 47% on warehouse-delivered snack foods at convenience stores in 2008.[4] This should not come as a surprise to consumers. A candy bar that might cost $.50 at a supermarket may cost $.75 (50% more) at a convenience store. Why? Undoubtedly, consumers do not make the trip to the convenience store to buy snack foods. In most cases, they enter the store to finalize a gasoline purchase. In deciding whether to buy the candy bar, the consumer is well aware that a better price can be had at a supermarket. But even if the candy bar is cheaper at the supermarket, the opportunity cost of buying it at the convenience store is fairly low, particularly when one considers the time involved in finding a better price. Therefore, we would expect consumers to be relatively price inelastic when it comes to goods that are relatively inexpensive.

Although consumers may claim that they're willing to pay the additional 50% for convenience, the rationale doesn't really hold up to scrutiny. Suppose a "convenient" auto dealer was selling a new car for $30,000 whereas a competing dealer on the other side of town was offering the identical car for $20,000. Would the consumer be willing to pay the additional 50% for the convenience? Clearly, the difference between paying 50% more for a candy bar as compared to 50% more for a new car is the opportunity cost of the purchase. Regardless of whether the consumer buys the car at the convenient dealership or the one across town, the opportunity cost of the purchase is sizable. Consequently, the higher the price as a percentage of the consumer's budget, the more price sensitive the consumer.

Orbitz discovered differences in the willingness to pay for hotels between Mac and PC users. Its own research showed that Mac users are willing to spend as much as 30% more on hotel rooms. Why? According to Forrester Research, the average income for Mac users is $98,560, as compared with an average income of $74,452 for PC users. The knowledge that Mac users were less price sensitive than PC users led Orbitz to steer potential customers who accessed the website on a Mac into pricier hotel rooms.

The final determinant of price elasticity is the time the consumer has to make a purchase. Consider an extreme case. The National Weather Service reports that a hurricane is imminent. When that occurs, coastal residents are in a rush to buy plywood shutters, install them quickly, and drive inland before the storm makes landfall. Under less trying circumstances, these same consumers would shop around for an acceptable price. With the hurricane due to arrive in a matter of hours, consumers have minimal opportunity to compare prices and may feel compelled to make a hasty purchase. Clearly, this gives a great deal more market power to the supplier of plywood, whose price need not be as competitive as it might have been during less urgent periods.

The importance of time as a determinant of price sensitivity should not be underestimated by firms. Because the price of a good represents opportunity cost, buyers seek ways to minimize the opportunity cost of a purchase. Firms that foolishly believe they have the advantage over consumers will eventually find that buyers found a way to lower their opportunity costs. When the price of gas increased by $.86/gallon between the spring of 2010 and 2011, both Toyota and Honda reported significant increases in Prius and Insight sales.[5] Clearly, most consumers are not in a position to buy a new car when gas prices rise. However, if fuel prices remain high, over time, consumers will look seriously at hybrids when they need a new vehicle. In summary, then, the longer the time the consumer has to make a purchase decision, the more elastic the demand for the good.

How can knowledge of price elasticity help a firm anticipate relevant revenues? To begin with, we need to find a way to measure price elasticity. Economists measure price elasticity as:

$$E_P = \% \text{ change in quantity purchased}/\% \text{ change in price}$$

In measuring price elasticity, note that "quantity purchased" is used instead of "quantity demanded." Although the intent is to equate the two, this may not always be the case. If the firm stocks out of an item, the quantity demanded may exceed the quantity purchased. For firms trying to measure price elasticity, this is an important consideration. If the quantity demanded exceeds the quantity purchased due to stockouts, the results may delude managers into thinking consumers are less price sensitive than they actually are.

Because the law of demand suggests that the quantity demanded decreases as prices rise, E_P is negative. The convention among many economists is to ignore the negative sign. In terms of measuring price elasticity, economists define "elastic" as any situation in which the percentage change in the quantity demanded exceeds the percentage change in the price. Based on the equation, then, if the good has a relatively elastic demand,

Table 3.4. *Measuring and Defining Elasticity*

1. If $E_P > 1$, demand is elastic (i.e. relatively responsive to price changes)
2. If $E_P < 1$, demand is inelastic (i.e. relatively unresponsive to price changes)
3. If $E_P = 1$, demand is unitary (i.e. percentage change in price equals percentage change in quantity)

the elasticity coefficient will be greater than one. For example, an elasticity coefficient of 2.5 means that each 1% change in the price leads to a 2.5% change in the quantity demanded. "Inelastic demand" is just the reverse: economists say that a good has a relatively inelastic demand if the percentage change in the quantity demanded is less than the percentage change in the price. In such cases, the elasticity coefficient will be less than one. For instance, if the elasticity coefficient is equal to 0.4, a 1% change in the price leads to a 0.4% change in the quantity demanded. If the percentage change in the quantity demanded is equal to the percentage change in the price (i.e. a 10% price increase leads to a 10% decrease in the quantity demanded), the good is exhibiting ***unitary*** elasticity. The definitions are summarized in Table 3.4.

The coefficient is more precisely measured as:

$$E_p = \frac{(\text{New quantity} - \text{old quantity}) / (\text{Average of the two quantities})}{(\text{New price} - \text{old price}) / (\text{Average of the two prices})}$$

Note that the respective denominators in calculating percentage changes are the average of the two quantities (or prices) rather than the original quantity (or price). This is to assure that the coefficient corresponding to a given price change along a demand curve will be the same regardless of whether the price increases or decreases. For example, suppose a firm increases the price from $5 to $11, and as a result, the quantity demanded decreases from six units to two units. If the percentage change in the price were measured as the change in the price divided by the original price, the percentage change would be equal to 120%. If, on the other hand, the price decreased from $11 to $5, the percentage change in the price would be equal to 54.5%. By dividing the price change by the average of the two prices, the percentage change will be the same regardless of whether the original price was $5 or $11.

When calculating the price elasticity of demand, firms should be cognizant of the fact that the two price/quantity combinations may not lie on the same demand curve. Figure 3.7 illustrates the problem that may arise. The graph on the left shows two price/quantity combinations. When using the numbers to calculate the price elasticity of demand, the firm assumes they lie on the same demand curve. In this example, when the price increased from $5 to $10, the firm witnesses a decline in unit sales from 100 units to 40 units. Plugging these numbers into the equation reveals:

$$E_p = \frac{(40-100)/70}{(\$10-\$5)/\$7.50} = -1.28 \left(\text{or } 1.28 \text{ if the negative sign is ignored}\right)$$

This suggests that demand is relatively elastic. Each 1% increase in the price led to a 1.28% decrease in the quantity demanded.

The graph on the right shows another possibility. One of the other determinants of demand may have changed; for example, the price of a substitute may have decreased. This would cause the demand curve to shift to the left. Had the price of the substitute remained unchanged, the quantity demanded would only have fallen to 80 units in response to the price increase. If so, the price elasticity coefficient would have been equal to:

$$E_p = \frac{(80-100)/90}{(\$10-\$5)/\$7.50} = -0.33 \text{ (or 0.33 if the negative sign is ignored)}$$

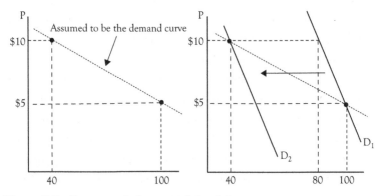

Figure 3.7. Incorrect inference of elasticity.

This suggests that demand is relatively inelastic. Each 1% increase in the price only led to a 0.33% decrease in the quantity demanded.

Unfortunately, the manager does not observe the 80 units that would have been sold if the price had increased to $10 and the price of the substitute had not changed. Because the price of the substitute did change, he only observes the 40 units that are sold. This misleads him into thinking consumers are more price sensitive than they actually are. One should note that the scenario on the right is likely to be encountered more often than not. Managers usually do not change prices randomly. Most of the time, the price change was motivated by a change in a factor that can shift a demand curve, such as the price charged by competing firms.

The relationship between price elasticity and revenue is important. For example, suppose a firm raises its price from $5 to $10 and the quantity demanded falls from 100 units to 60 units. In this case, raising the price caused the firm's revenue to increase from $500 to $600. Suppose, however, that in response to the price increase, the quantity demanded falls from 100 units to 40 units. In this circumstance, the price increase caused revenues to fall from $500 to $400. Figure 3.8 illustrates the distinction. Note that the demand curve that corresponds to the decrease in revenues is more elastic than the demand curve that is associated with an increase in revenues.

When we reflect on the definitions of elastic and inelastic in Table 3.4, the relationship between elasticity and revenue should become fairly

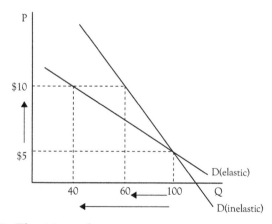

Figure 3.8. Elasticity and revenue.

obvious. We define demand as "elastic" if the percentage change in quantity exceeds the percentage change in price. If, for example, the price rises by 10%, the quantity demanded will fall by more than 10%, which implies that revenue will decrease. If, on the other hand, the price declines by 10%, the quantity demanded will rise by more than 10%. This suggests that revenues will increase in response to the price cut. In general, when the demand is elastic, price and revenue will move in opposite directions.

If demand is relatively inelastic, the percentage change in the quantity demanded will be less than the percentage change in the price. Thus, if the price rises by 10%, the quantity demanded will fall by less than 10%, causing revenue to rise. If the price falls by 10%, the quantity demanded will rise by less than 10%, leading to a decrease in revenue. If demand is inelastic, therefore, price and revenue will move in the same direction.

Finally, if demand is unitary, a given percentage change in the price will lead to an identical percentage change in the quantity demanded. For example, a 10% price hike will lead to a 10% decline in the quantity demanded. The two percentage changes cancel out, causing revenues to remain the same. Table 3.5 summarizes the relationship between elasticity and revenue.

Apple Corporation's iTunes illustrated the relationship between price elasticity and revenue when it increased the price of many of its songs from $.99 to $1.29 in 2009. One day after the price increase, 60 songs on its top 100 charts carried a price of $1.29 whereas the remaining 40 were still priced at $.99. In 24 hours, the $1.29 songs lost an average of 5.3 positions in the charts while the $.99 songs gained an average of 2.5 positions. The data revealed that the number of downloads for songs whose prices had been raised fell relative to those whose prices remained at $.99.

Table 3.5. Relationship Between Elasticity and Revenue

1. Elastic	% change in QD > % change in P	Price and revenue move in opposite directions
2. Inelastic	% change in QD < % change in P	Price and revenue move in the same direction
3. Unitary	% change in QD = % change in P	Revenue will not change if the price changes

But did fewer downloads translate into more or less revenue? According to Nielsen Soundscan data, a #42 song is downloaded roughly 9,800 times over a two-day period.[6] At a price of $.99, the song generates $9,702 over that time span. In contrast, a #45 song is downloaded approximately 9,200 times over two days. At a retail price of $1.29, the song generates $11,868 over two days. Hence, if raising the price from $.99 to $1.29 causes the number of downloads to fall from 9,800 to 9,200 over a two-day period, revenues rise by over $2,000. In general, downloads would have to drop by more than 23% for the price increase to cause revenues to fall.

Although many persons (economists included) tend to label a good as having either an elastic demand or an inelastic demand, the elasticity for a linear demand curve depends on the price. If we examine the demand schedule in Table 3.6 and calculate the price elasticity of demand between each pair of prices, the results are illuminating.

As Table 3.6 indicates, the price elasticity of demand is not constant across all prices. Between $3 and $5, demand is inelastic. Between $5 and $6, demand is unitary, and demand is elastic for prices above $6. We can also see that as we move up the demand curve, the coefficient becomes increasingly elastic.

This revelation should not be too surprising. We used snack foods at a convenience store to illustrate why the price of snack foods could be 50% higher than at a supermarket without causing sales to suffer dramatically.

Table 3.6. Price Elasticities Along the Demand Curve

Price	Quantity	Elasticity coefficient
$8	3	
		2.14
$7	4	
		1.44
$6	5	
		1
$5	6	
		0.69
$4	7	
		0.47
$3	8	

Let's assume that the manager of the store increased the price of a candy bar from $.50 to $.75. Although the number of candy bars sold decreased revenues increased. This would indicate that the candy bars had an inelastic demand. The manager would be foolish to believe that candy bars would have an inelastic demand at all prices. If consumers were relatively insensitive to candy bar prices, and price increases were inevitably accompanied by rising revenue, then charging $25 for a candy bar would yield far greater revenues than $.75. Clearly, the store would be hard pressed to sell *any* candy bars at a price of $25. It stands to reason, then, that somewhere between $.75 and $25, the demand goes from being inelastic to elastic.

Let's see how the relationship between elasticity and the demand curve affects relevant revenue. Theory suggests that demand tends to be relatively inelastic at lower prices, becomes unitary at a higher price, and eventually becomes elastic at even higher prices. Earlier, we stated that if the current price is in the inelastic portion of a demand curve, an increase in the price will cause revenues to rise. On the other hand, if the current price is in the elastic section of the demand curve, decreasing the price will cause revenues to rise. Understanding price elasticity is clearly important when one attempts to estimate the relevant revenue associated with a price change.

However, we can take theory one step further. If price increases in the inelastic section cause revenue to rise, and price cuts in the elastic section also cause revenue to rise, the firm will maximize revenues by setting its price in the unitary section of the demand curve. This is shown in Figure 3.9. As the price moves toward P^*, revenues rise. Total revenues

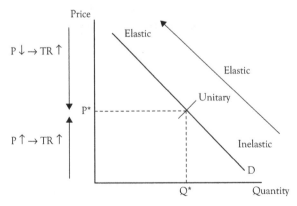

Figure 3.9. Elasticity and the revenue-maximizing price.

are maximized by setting the price in the unitary section of the demand curve. At that price, Q^* units are demanded.

Of course, firms are interested in maximizing profits, not revenues. Although an understanding of price elasticity is critical to the decision maker, the scenario exhibited in Figure 3.9 will also maximize profits if the firm has no variable costs. This is likely to be the case for setting ticket prices. The seats already exist; the relevant decision is what price to charge. Because variable costs will not change as more tickets are sold, the firm seeks the ticket price that will maximize revenues. In doing so, it will also maximize profits. Note that in this context, the ticket seller may actually be more profitable by leaving seats empty than by lowering the price to assure a sellout.

Cross-Price Elasticity of Demand

Another concept that is critical to anticipating relevant revenue is the **cross-price elasticity of demand**. Often, a firm may offer complementary or substitute goods in its product lines. At Burger King, French fries and soft drinks are complements to hamburgers. Proctor and Gamble's line of laundry detergents include Tide, Cheer, and Bold. Although they are all P&G brands, consumers view them as substitutes. When a firm has product lines that serve as either complements or substitutes for other lines, a change in the price of one good might affect the unit sales of the other good. An increase in the price of hamburgers at Burger King may decrease not only the quantity of hamburgers demanded, but also the quantity of fries demanded. This is illustrated in Figure 3.10.

The cross-price elasticity of demand is a means to measure the sensitivity of unit sales of one good to changes in the price of a related good. It is calculated as:

E_C = % change in the quantity of good Y purchased/% change in the
    P of good X,

where goods X and Y are either substitutes or complements. In evaluating the coefficient, the primary difference between the cross-price elasticity of demand and the standard price elasticity coefficient is that the latter is, by definition negative (price and quantity are inversely related on the demand

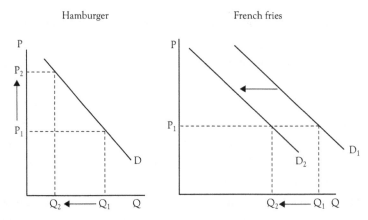

Figure 3.10. Cross-price elasticity of demand.

curve). Therefore, economists usually ignore the negative sign. In contrast, the cross-price elasticity of demand can be either positive or negative, depending on the relationship between X and Y. If the two goods are complementary, an increase in the price of X will cause the unit sales of Y to fall, implying a negative cross-elasticity coefficient. For example, if the estimated cross-elasticity coefficient is –3, a 1% increase in the price of X will lead to a 3% decrease in the unit sales of the complementary product. If X and Y are substitutes, an increase in the price of X will result in increased unit sales of Y. In this case, the cross-elasticity coefficient will be positive. As an example, a cross-elasticity coefficient of 0.85 implies that a 1% increase in the price of X will cause the unit sales of the substitute good, Y, to increase by 0.85%.

The cross-elasticity coefficient can be useful to determine the degree of complementarity or substitutability across product lines. Suppose, for example, that the cross-elasticity coefficient that measures the responsiveness of French fry sales to changes in hamburger prices is –4. In contrast, suppose the coefficient that measures the responsiveness of ice cream sundaes to changes in hamburger prices is –0.10. The first scenario implies that each 1% increase in the price of hamburgers decreases the quantity of French fries sold by 4% whereas, in the second case, a 1% increase in the price of hamburgers causes ice cream sundae sales to fall by 0.10%. Together, these coefficients imply that fries are a much closer complement to hamburger sales than are ice cream sundae sales.

The same type of comparisons can be made for product lines that are potentially substitutes for each other. The cross-elasticity coefficient that measures the responsiveness of chicken sandwich sales to changes in hamburger prices may be 1.5, whereas the responsiveness of salad sales to changes in hamburger prices may be 0.3. One would infer from these coefficients that chicken sandwiches are considered by customers to be closer substitutes for hamburgers than salads.

In anticipating relevant revenue, firms need to be cognizant of how a price/production decision for one good might affect the unit sales of related goods in their product lines. If the firm lowers the price for one good, the increase in unit sales will be accompanied by rising unit sales in complementary goods. Hence, the relevant revenue would be equal to the sum of the output and price effects for the product whose price has changed, plus the additional revenue generated for its complement.

On the other hand, if the product line includes substitutes, the relevant revenue from a price cut will be less than the marginal revenue from the good in question. Any price decrease aimed at increasing unit sales for one good will cannibalize some of the unit sales for the substitute good in the firm's product line. Hence, the relevant revenue will be the sum of the output and price effects for the good in question less the loss in revenue from declining unit sales for the substitute good.

Summary

- The law of demand states that as the price of a good rises, the quantity demanded decreases. This means that to sell more units, firms will have to lower prices.
- The relevant revenue in production decisions is called marginal revenue. Marginal revenue associated with a production increase is the sum of the output and price effects. The output effect is the revenue generated by the additional units sold. The price effect is the lost revenue due to dropping the price on the other units.
- Changes in other factors can cause demand to increase or decrease. Changes in incomes, prices of substitutes, prices of complementary goods, consumer tastes, and price expectations may allow the firm to sell more units or fewer units at the same price.

- Price elasticity measures the responsiveness of the quantity demanded to changes in the price. If the percentage change in the quantity demanded exceeds the percentage change in the price, demand is elastic. If the percentage change in the quantity demanded is less than the percentage change in the price, demand is inelastic. If the percentage change in the quantity demanded is equal to the percentage change in the price, demand is unitary.
- Price elasticity is determined by whether the good is a luxury or a necessity, the availability of substitutes, the definition of the market, the price of the good as a percentage of the buyer's budget, and the time the buyer has to make a purchase.
- Price elasticity is measured as: (New quantity – old quantity)/ (average of the quantities) divided by (New price – old price)/ (average of the prices). The coefficient reports the percentage change in the quantity demanded resulting from a 1% change in the price. If the ratio exceeds 1, demand is elastic. If the ratio is less than 1, demand is inelastic. If the ratio is equal to 1, demand is unitary.
- The higher the price of the good, the more elastic the demand. At lower prices, demand is inelastic. As the price rises, demand becomes unitary. As the price continues to rise, demand becomes elastic. Revenues are maximized by setting the price in the unitary section of the demand curve.
- The cross-elasticity of demand measures the responsiveness of the quantity demanded of one good to price changes in a related good. In terms of relevant revenues, firms should be cognizant as to how price changes will affect the unit sales of substitute or complementary goods in their product line.

CHAPTER 4

What Your Cost Accountant Can't Measure: The Economic Theory of Production and Cost

Having determined the relevant revenue associated with a decision, the manager must determine relevant cost. The critical theme of this book is that cost accounting methods rarely report the unit cost figure relevant to the manager's decision.

We might begin by asking what "unit cost" means. Marketing managers, for example, would be ill-advised to make pricing decisions without knowing what it would cost to produce the output. Although one might ask a cost accountant to define unit cost, it is more telling to pose it to the decision maker. The name "unit cost" implies the cost of making a unit of output. Therefore, if told that unit cost is $15, the individual in charge of pricing would likely conclude that the firm cannot charge a price less than $15 without incurring a loss from the sale of the good.

But this is not necessarily the case. Recall our definition of relevant costs in Chapter 2. Sunk costs refer to expenses that will be incurred regardless of whether the decision is implemented. For that reason, they are never relevant to the decision and should be ignored. In our example, suppose $5 of the $15 unit cost estimate is sunk. If that was the case, any price above $10 would add to the firm's profits. But how likely is the manager to conclude that he can charge a price as low as $10 without incurring a loss? A more likely scenario is that the manager will incorrectly infer that the entire $15 is relevant, which might cause him to make a pricing error.

Let's address the definition of unit cost in another example. Suppose the firm has produced three units and is considering a fourth. The manager knows it can sell the unit for $500 and sees that unit cost is equal to $400. Should the firm produce the additional unit? At first glance, the answer appears to be obvious: if the unit cost is $400 and can be sold for $500, it will add $100 to the firm's profits.

In all likelihood, the unit cost figure reported to the manager is not the cost of producing the fourth unit, but the *average cost* of producing four units. Suppose, in fact, that the first unit costs $250 to produce, the second costs $350, the third costs $450, and the fourth unit costs $550 to produce. Indeed, the cost of producing four units sums to $1,600, which implies an average of $400/unit. But the unit under consideration costs $550 to produce. If the firm produces the unit and sells it for $500, its profits will *fall* by $50.

We can relate this latter case to relevant revenue and relevant cost. The unit cost estimate supplied by the cost accountant may be $400, but the relevant cost incurred by producing the fourth unit is $550. This is why selling the fourth unit for $500 causes the firm to incur a loss.

Why didn't the cost accountant simply report the unit cost to be $550? In all likelihood, the cost accountant does not know the cost of producing each unit individually because it simply cannot be known with certainty. If a firm produces 10,000 units/day, does it know the cost of producing *each individual unit*? Or is it in a better position to estimate the average cost/unit over a range of 10,000 units, knowing that the cost of each individual unit may vary? "Unit cost" as estimated by cost accounting rarely reports the cost of producing *each individual unit*, but rather, the average costs incurred over a range of production. But, as our simple example illustrated, the manager who relied on the $400 unit cost estimate to sell the fourth unit for $500 made the wrong decision.

This establishes the focus of this chapter. We will rely on microeconomic principles to derive the economic theory of cost. This will illustrate what the cost accountant would measure in a world of perfect information. In the subsequent chapter, we will review the most commonly used cost accounting methods and how the unit cost estimates may differ from what the manager needs to know. Most importantly, we will be able to see how the imperfections in unit cost estimates can bias the decisions of managers.

Production Theory

Cost theory is derived from the theory of production. To illustrate, assume a worker is paid a wage of $10/hour and the direct materials expense associated with each unit is $5. If the worker is capable of producing one unit per hour, then the unit cost is $15. Suppose the worker is capable of producing two units per hour. In that case, total production costs for the hour are $20 ($10 for direct labor and $10 for direct materials), leading to a unit cost of $10. Note that when the worker became more productive, unit cost decreased. Let's develop a theory that is sufficiently general as to describe patterns experienced by most firms. Later, we will use the theory to derive a theory of costs.

Mary started a doughnut shop. She rents a space in a small shopping plaza for $1,000/month. She purchased a doughnut fryer for $6,000. A fryer is capable of producing up to 180 doughnuts per hour. For loading and unloading doughnuts, she bought a proofer for $4,000 and $2,000 for a glazing table. Mary spent an additional $15,000 refurbishing the restaurant for sit-down customers.

When the business was just getting started, she hired one worker to make the doughnuts while she operated the cash register. Once the worker learned the ropes, she found he was capable of producing 40 doughnuts per hour. As the popularity of the business grew, Mary found that one worker was insufficient as a bottle-neck of customers appeared at peak morning hours. She hired a second worker to help make the doughnuts. Had the two workers worked individually, and assuming they had equal ability, they could collectively make 80 doughnuts per hour. However, the workers found they could produce more doughnuts by taking on more specialized tasks, thereby divvying up the responsibilities. In doing so, they could produce 100 doughnuts per hour.

As the business grew, Mary needed to add a third worker. As the workers continued to divvy up the responsibilities to maximize production, they found that with three workers, 130 doughnuts could be produced per hour. When three workers proved to be insufficient, she hired a fourth worker. With four workers, an average of 150 doughnuts per hour could be produced. Eventually, Mary settled on five workers, who collectively averaged 160 doughnuts per hour.

Let's review the pattern between labor hours and production. *Total product* refers to the total output produced within a given time frame. We begin with the logical assumption that no doughnuts would have been produced without labor. Table 4.1 indicates the total product associated with each quantity of labor hours. As one would expect, doughnut production increases as the number of labor hours rises.[1]

Figure 4.1 graphs the total product curve. Notice that although doughnut production is positively related to the number of labor hours used, it does not follow a linear pattern.

To understand why total product does not follow a straight line, we will develop another measurement called *marginal product*. Marginal product refers to the additional output generated by an additional input. Examine the marginal product of each labor hour. The first labor hour results in 40 additional doughnuts. The second labor hour causes

Table 4.1. Total Product

Labor hours	Total product
0	0
1	40
2	100
3	130
4	150
5	160

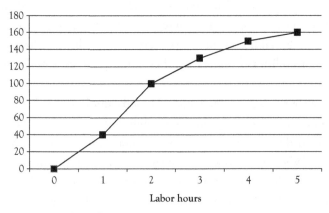

Figure 4.1. Total product.

doughnut production to rise from 40 to 100, an increase of 60 doughnuts. As noted earlier, had the second worker produced the doughnuts on his own, and assuming he had identical skills to the first worker, doughnut production would have risen by another 40 doughnuts. However, the workers recognized the benefits from specialization; that more doughnuts could be produced each hour by divvying up responsibilities rather than having each person work individually. Economic theory assumes this pattern exists in most production settings: initially, as workers specialize, the marginal product of each additional worker rises.

Note, however, that the pattern of rising marginal product comes to an abrupt halt beginning with the third worker. When the third worker comes aboard, the number of doughnuts produced each hour rises from 100 to 130, or by 30 doughnuts. This is less than the number of doughnuts added by the second worker. Economists refer to this as the ***law of diminishing marginal returns***. The law states that as additional inputs are added to production, eventually each input results in less additional production.

The law has nothing to do with the worker's ability. In fact, we assume throughout our analysis that the workers are equally skilled. Rather, it's just a matter of numbers. As an analogy, consider a person who is moving out of an apartment and must carry a sleeper sofa. The sofa is large and awkward, so it would likely take a long time for a single individual to carry it outside to a moving van. If the person had a helper, they would likely grab opposite ends of the sofa and carry it to the van in less than half the time. This is an example of rising marginal product. Suppose a third person helped. Three persons might be able to carry the sofa to the van faster than two persons could, but the third person's contribution would probably be smaller than that of the second helper. This would constitute an example of diminishing returns.

In the doughnut shop example, although the individuals are trying to work together cohesively, they have to share the workspace and equipment. Production rises with the third worker, but his marginal contribution is smaller than that of either of the first two workers. We can see the diminishing returns with additional workers as well, as the fourth worker adds 20 doughnuts and the fifth worker adds 10. Table 4.2 derives the marginal product associated with each labor hour.

Table 4.2. Marginal Product

Labor hours	Total product	Marginal product
0	0	–
1	40	40
2	100	60
3	130	30
4	150	20
5	160	10

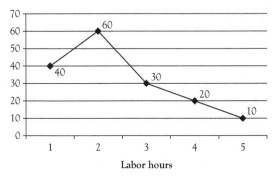

Figure 4.2. Marginal product.

Figure 4.2 plots the marginal product information. The graph clearly indicates that the second worker adds more to total production than the first worker, and that the law of diminishing marginal returns sets in with the third worker.

The final measurement of labor productivity is called ***average product***. It measures the average output per input (in this case, the average output per labor hour). Table 4.3 calculates the average product associated with each quantity of labor hours. It is simply the total product divided by the number of labor hours.

Note how the average product compares with marginal product for each quantity of labor hours. The two measurements are the same for one labor hour. The first labor hour adds 40 doughnuts to total production, resulting in an average of 40 doughnuts per labor hour.

But note how the two numbers deviate from that point forward. The second labor hour adds 60 doughnuts, causing the average number of doughnuts per labor hour to rise to 50. In general, when the marginal

Table 4.3. Average Product

Labor hours	Total product	Marginal product	Average product
0	0	–	–
1	40	40	40
2	100	60	50
3	130	30	43.33
4	150	20	37.50
5	160	10	32

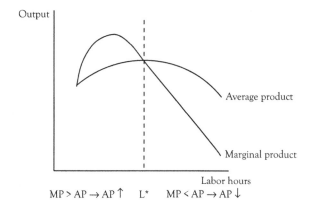

$$MP > AP \to AP \uparrow \quad L^* \quad MP < AP \to AP \downarrow$$

Figure 4.3. Graph of a marginal product and average product curve.

product exceeds the average product, average product will rise. This is analogous to a student's cumulative GPA and his most recent semester's GPA. If his cumulative GPA is 3.00 and he earns a 3.25 in his next semester, his cumulative average will rise. In the doughnut example, the average number of doughnuts produced in one labor hour is 40. Because the second labor hour contributes more than 40 doughnuts, the average product will rise (to 50/hour in this example).

Note how the average product declines when the marginal product is below the average. The average number of doughnuts produced over two hours is 50. Because the third labor hour contributes only 30 doughnuts, the average falls to 43.33.

Figure 4.3 shows a generic graph of the marginal and average product curves. The average product has the shape of an inverted U: as the number of labor hours increases, the average number of units produced per labor hour rises, reaches a maximum when the average product is equal to marginal product, and then begins to decline. More specifically, as long as the marginal product exceeds the average product, the average product will continue to rise. As soon as the marginal product is less than the average product, the average product will begin to fall.

Cost Theory

Total Fixed and Total Variable Cost

We will use production theory to derive a theory of costs. Before applying production theory, we need to recall the distinction between **fixed costs** and **variable costs**. Fixed costs are expenses that do not vary with output. In the doughnut example, the $1,000 monthly rent is an ongoing fixed cost.[2]

Variable costs are expenses that vary with production. Wages are a variable cost because the number of doughnuts produced varies with the number of labor hours used. The costs of the ingredients that go into each doughnut (flour, yeast, sugar, etc.) are also variable costs. Suppose each worker is paid $10/hour, including benefits and worker's compensation. Ingredients expenses average $.12/doughnut. Because our only ongoing fixed cost is paid by the month, we will adapt the hourly production information in Table 4.4 to derive the total variable costs associated with each quantity of doughnuts produced each month (assuming eight hours/day, six days/week, four weeks/month).

We know that one worker can produce 40 doughnuts per hour. If that individual works eight hours/day, six days/week for four weeks, 7,680

Table 4.4. Monthly Total Variable Costs

Total product	Direct labor	Direct materials	Total variable cost
0	$0	$0	$0
7,680	$1,920	$922	$2,842
19,200	$3,840	$2,304	$6,144
24,960	$5,760	$2,995	$8,755
28,800	$7,680	$3,456	$11,136
30,720	$9,600	$3,686	$13,286

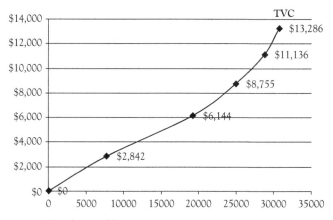

Figure 4.4. Total variable costs.

doughnuts will be produced each month. The direct labor cost will be $10/hour × 192 hours, or $1,920. The direct materials cost will be 7,680 doughnuts × $.12/doughnut, or $922. The total variable cost associated with producing 7,680 doughnuts is $2,842. Two workers can produce 100 doughnuts/hour or 19,200/month. Direct labor expenses will equal $10/hour × 192 hours × two workers or $3,840. Direct materials expenses will be equal to $.12/doughnut × 19,200 doughnuts, or $2,304. Thus, the total variable cost of producing 19,200 doughnuts will be $6,144. The remainder of the table shows the costs associated with the doughnuts produced by three, four, and five workers.

A graph of the doughnut shop's total variable costs appears in Figure 4.4. As the graph illustrates, the firm's total variable costs rise as the number of doughnuts produced increases.

If we sum the total fixed and total variable costs together, we get the total cost associated with each quantity of doughnuts. This is shown in Table 4.5. Note that the firm's total costs begin with the total fixed cost and rise as the quantity of output rises. A graph of the total cost data, combined with the total variable and total fixed cost appears in Figure 4.5.

Average Fixed and Variable Cost

Many product-related decisions are based on estimates of unit costs. Let's take the data for the doughnut shop and convert them into average costs.

Table 4.5. Total Fixed, Total Variable, and Total Cost

Total product	Total fixed cost	Total variable cost	Total cost
0	$1,000	$0	$1,000
7,680	$1,000	$2,842	$3,842
19,200	$1,000	$6,144	$7,144
24,960	$1,000	$8,755	$9,755
28,800	$1,000	$11,136	$12,136
30,720	$1,000	$13,286	$14,286

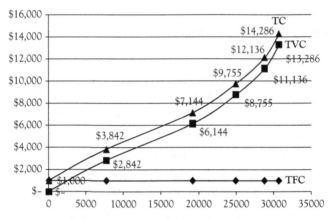

Figure 4.5. Total fixed, total variable, and total cost curves.

First, let's derive the **average fixed cost** which measures the fixed cost per doughnut. As noted earlier, the shop incurs $1,000 in monthly fixed costs. If we divide $1,000 by the number of doughnuts produced each month, we can determine the average fixed cost. As Table 4.6 indicates, the average fixed cost declines as more doughnuts are produced. This should be fairly intuitive: because total fixed costs do not change with production, the fixed cost per doughnut decreases as more doughnuts are produced. A graph of the average fixed cost data appears in Figure 4.6.

The notion that average fixed cost decreases as production increases is not particularly insightful, nor is it very useful for decision making. A more useful measure is the **average variable cost,** or the variable cost per unit. Because variable costs are incurred each time a unit is produced, it is critical that managers charge a price that will at least cover this cost. Average variable cost is calculated by dividing the total variable cost by the number

Table 4.6. Average Fixed Cost

Total product	Average fixed cost
0	–
7,680	$0.130
19,200	$0.052
24,960	$0.040
28,800	$0.035
30,720	$0.033

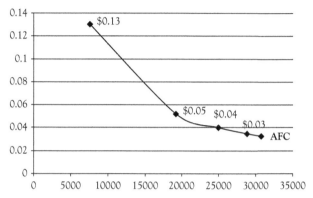

Figure 4.6. Average fixed cost.

of units produced. Based on the doughnut data, the average variable cost at each output level appears in Table 4.7.

The graph of the average variable cost data appears in Figure 4.7. Note that the average variable cost is U shaped. As production rises, the variable expense per unit declines at first, but eventually rises. The U shape of average variable cost can be traced to the inverted U shape of average product. We noted that as more labor hours were employed, the average output per labor hour increased, reached a maximum, and then declined. This helps one to see the relationship between average product and average variable cost. If the average output per labor hour rises, the average labor expense per unit necessarily decreases. As an analogy, consider the relationship between gas mileage (a.k.a. the average productivity of your car) and the gasoline cost per mile (a.k.a. average variable cost). As your miles per gallon increases, your gasoline cost per mile decreases, and vice versa. The same is true in production: as average product rises, average

Table 4.7. Average Variable Cost

Total product	Total variable cost	Average variable cost
0	$0	–
7,680	$2,842	$0.37
19,200	$6,144	$0.32
24,960	$8,755	$0.35
28,800	$11,136	$0.39
30,720	$13,286	$0.43

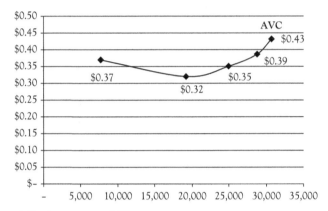

Figure 4.7. Average variable cost.

variable cost falls. Likewise, as average product declines, average variable costs rise.

If we sum the average fixed and average variable costs, we get the ***average total cost***, or the average total expenditure per unit. Table 4.8 shows that as output rises, average total cost decreases. In fact, this is only true up to a point. We know that as output rises, average fixed cost continually decreases while average variable cost falls initially, but eventually rises. But as production continues to rise, average fixed cost becomes negligible.

Noting that average total cost eventually rises as production increases, Figure 4.8 combines the average fixed and average variable cost curves from Figures 4.6 and 4.7 and adds the average total cost data. Whereas average fixed cost steadily declines with production, average variable cost and average total cost exhibit a U shape.

Table 4.8. *Average Variable Cost*

Total product	Average fixed cost	Average variable cost	Average total cost
0	–	–	–
7,680	$0.130	$0.37	$0.50
19,200	$0.052	$0.32	$0.37
24,960	$0.040	$0.35	$0.39
28,800	$0.035	$0.39	$0.42
30,720	$0.033	$0.43	$0.47

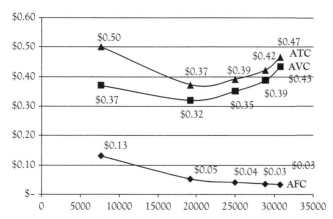

Figure 4.8. Average fixed cost, average variable cost, and average total cost.

Marginal Cost

The most important measure of unit cost is **marginal cost**. Marginal cost is the additional cost of producing an additional unit of output. To illustrate its importance, suppose someone approaches a contractor about building a house. He's selected the house from a book of housing plans and presents it to the contractor. Before they go ahead with the construction, the contractor must provide the individual with a quote. Knowing that the person is likely to solicit quotes from competing contractors, the quote must cover the cost of the construction and offer an acceptable profit. If the contractor quotes too high a price, a competing contractor may undercut him. If the quote is too low, the contractor may lose money on the house.

**Table 4.9. Hourly Doughnut Shop
Variable Costs**

Total product	Total variable cost
0	$0
40	$14.80
100	$32
130	$45.60
150	$58
160	$69.20

Marginal cost in this context is the cost of producing this house. It does not serve the interests of the contractor to base his quote on the cost of building the average house, given that this house may be more or less expensive to build than the average house. Likewise, it does not serve the contractor to base his quote on the cost of identical houses in the past if lumber prices have been rising.

Let's review the data for the doughnut shop and demonstrate why marginal cost is difficult to measure with certainty. Table 4.9 shows the hourly variable costs associated with each quantity of doughnuts. We focus only on variable costs because fixed costs do not vary with the number of doughnuts produced.

Examining the table, what is the marginal cost of the 80th doughnut? The table does not show us. We know the cost of making 40 doughnuts and the cost of making 100 doughnuts, but we do not know the cost of making the 80th doughnut. The table only allows us to measure changes in total costs that occur across discrete changes in production. For example, we know that increasing production from zero doughnuts to 40 doughnuts causes expenses to rise by $14.80. We also know that increasing production from 40 doughnuts to 100 doughnuts causes the shop's operating costs to rise by $17.20.

Although the table does not reveal the marginal cost of the 80th doughnut, let's manipulate the data to get the best estimate we can. Table 4.10 creates a new column that shows the change in total variable cost divided by the change in production.

As the table indicates, the change in total variable cost resulting from a given change in production varies. But let's go back to our previous

Table 4.10. Problems in Estimating Marginal Cost

Total product	Total variable cost	Change in total variable cost/change in production
0	$0	
40	$14.80	($14.80 – $0)/40 = $.37
100	$32	($32 – $14.80)/60 = $.29
130	$45.60	($45.60 – $32)/30 = $.45
150	$58	($58 – $45.60)/20 = $.62
160	$69.20	($69.20 – $58)/10 = $1.12

question: what is the marginal cost of the 80th doughnut? As the table indicates, we still don't know. All we really know is that the average cost of producing doughnuts 41 through 100 is $.29. But does that mean that each of those doughnuts cost exactly $.29 to produce?

The table suggests that this is unlikely because the costs differ between production levels. The average cost of the first 40 doughnuts is $.37 and the average cost of doughnuts 101–130 is $.45. If the average cost across production levels differs, it is quite likely that the cost of each unit within a given production level will vary as well.

If we define marginal cost as the cost of producing each individual unit, we can see that Table 4.10 doesn't really report marginal cost. Instead, the numbers reveal the average variable cost within discrete levels of production. If the *average* doughnut between 40 and 100 costs $.29 to make, some of those doughnuts have a marginal cost that is less than $.29 and some of them have a marginal cost that is greater than $.29.

This illustrates the problem that cost accountants face when measuring unit cost. It also affects managers who rely on unit cost estimates to make decisions. Most cost accounting methods report unit cost estimates similar to those that appear in Table 4.10. But because the true marginal cost of each unit is unknown, managers rely on the average variable cost measure as the *best estimate* of the marginal cost of each unit.

Why might this be problematic? Let's incorporate demand analysis. Suppose 80 doughnuts are demanded at a price of $.40. Should the doughnut shop set its price at $.40 and produce 80 doughnuts? The doughnut shop does not have precise information that allows it to estimate the marginal cost of each individual doughnut. Table 4.10 states that the average cost of producing doughnuts 41–100 is $.29, but we know that each of those doughnuts does not cost exactly $.29 to produce. Given that the average variable cost of doughnuts 101–130 is $.45, the marginal cost of each doughnut must begin to rise somewhere between 41 and 100. Any doughnut that costs more than $.40 to produce will be sold at a loss. But the doughnut shop lacks the necessary data to determine which doughnuts can be sold profitably for $.40 and which cannot.

If we examine Table 4.10, we see that the change in total variable costs divided by the change in output falls initially, but then rises. Let's combine the numbers in the table with economic theory to explain the likely patterns in marginal cost. Earlier, we noted that average variable cost was the mirror image of average product: if the average output per labor hour was rising, the average labor cost per unit must be falling. The same relationship exists between marginal product and marginal cost. If the marginal productivity of a labor hour rises, the marginal cost of the output produced must decrease. This point was made in the example at the beginning of the chapter. When the marginal product of the worker increased from one unit/hour to two units/hour, the marginal cost of the units decreased from $15 to $10.

Economic theory suggests that marginal product rises initially, but then falls once the law of diminishing returns sets in. If marginal cost follows the inverse pattern of marginal product, the marginal cost of each unit falls initially, but eventually rises. Figure 4.9 shows a graph of the marginal product curve and its corresponding marginal cost curve. As the figure illustrates, marginal cost is at its lowest when marginal product is at its highest. More importantly, the figure shows that for the most part, marginal cost is rising. This implies that once diminishing returns set in, each unit costs more to produce than the previous unit.

The Profit-Maximizing Price and Output

Let's incorporate a demand schedule and combine it with the cost data to determine the optimal price and output level. Table 4.11 shows the firm's demand and cost schedules.

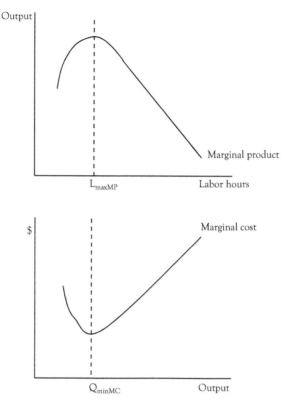

Figure 4.9. Graph of a marginal product and marginal cost curve.

Table 4.11. The Profit-Maximizing Price and Output

Price	Quantity	Total revenue	Relevant revenue	Total variable cost	Revenue cost
	0	$0	–	$0	–
$1	40	$40	$40	$14.80	$14.80
$.90	100	$90	$50	$32	$17.20
$.75	130	$97.50	$7.50	$45.60	$13.60
$.60	150	$90	($7.50)	$58	$12.40
$.40	160	$64	($26)	$69.20	$11.20

We can approach the firm's profit-maximizing price and output using relevant revenue/relevant cost analysis. The first decision Mary must make is whether to produce the first 40 doughnuts (i.e. the production generated by the first worker). The relevant revenue is the amount by which revenue changes if the doughnuts are produced, or $40. The costs will increase by $14.80. Therefore, the profit generated by the doughnut shop each hour will rise by $25.20.

Next, Mary must decide whether to hire another worker to assist the first one. If the second worker is hired, hourly doughnut production will rise from 40 to 100. Because more doughnuts will be produced, the law of demand will require Mary to drop the price from $1 to $.90 to assure they will all be sold. As the table indicates, increasing hourly production from 40 doughnuts to 100 will cause revenues to rise by $50 whereas costs increase by $17.20. Hourly profits will rise by $32.80 if the additional 60 doughnuts per hour are produced.

Should hourly production rise to 130? The law of demand suggests that if hourly production increases to 130, Mary will have to drop the price to $.75. This will cause revenues to increase by $7.50. However, costs will rise by $13.60. If Mary hires the third worker, the shop's profits will decline by $6.10 per hour. This implies that profits are highest when 100 doughnuts are produced per hour, and priced at $.90/doughnut.

Let's take the same analysis and look at it from the perspective of changes in revenue per unit and changes in costs per unit. In other words, we are comparing marginal revenue and our best available estimate of marginal cost. Table 4.12 adapts the information in Table 4.11.

As the table indicates, the first 40 doughnuts will generate an average of $1/doughnut in additional revenues while adding an average of $.37/doughnut to costs. This suggests that the first 40 doughnuts will add to Mary's profits. The next 60 doughnuts generate an additional $.83/

Table 4.12. Marginal Revenue/Marginal Cost Analysis

Price	Quantity	Total revenue	Marginal revenue (change in TR/ change in Q)	Total variable cost	Marginal cost estimate (change in TVC/ change in Q)
	0	$0	–	$0	–
$1	40	$40	$1	$14.80	$.37
$.90	100	$90	$.83	$32	$.29
$.75	130	$97.50	$.25	$45.60	$.45
$.60	150	$90	($.38)	$58	$.62
$.40	160	$64	($2.60)	$69.20	$1.12 .

doughnut in revenue, while adding $.29/doughnut to the shop's costs. On average, these doughnuts will also add to the shop's profits. Mary should not increase production to 130. If she does, the additional revenue per doughnut ($.25) is less than the added cost ($.45).

But we've already noted that the cost figures in Table 4.12 do not accurately report marginal cost. Instead, they report average variable cost between discrete output levels. Even so, the table provides insights that we will use to derive a theory of profit maximization if marginal cost was known. The analysis suggests that each doughnut whose marginal revenue exceeds its marginal cost will add to the shop's profits. If the marginal cost of the doughnut is greater than its marginal revenue, the doughnut will decrease the firm's profits. Demand theory suggests that marginal revenue gradually declines as production increases, while marginal cost increases with production after diminishing returns sets in. Therefore, Mary will eventually reach a point that the marginal cost of producing additional doughnuts exceeds the marginal revenue. Increasing production into this range will cause profits to fall.

Figure 4.10 shows the implications of marginal revenue/marginal cost analysis using demand and cost theory. The firm will produce every unit for which the marginal revenue is greater than the marginal cost, but will not produce any unit for which the marginal cost exceeds the marginal revenue. As the figure indicates, the firm will maximize its profits by producing Q^* units. Given the law of demand, the highest price that will allow Q^* units to be sold is P^*. No other price/quantity combination will be more profitable.

This brings us back to our original point. Figure 4.10 illustrates what the firm wishes to do. Its goal is to determine the price/output level that will maximize profits. In other words, each firm wants to identify P^* and Q^*. But cost accounting does not report marginal cost. Instead, average variable cost estimates are frequently used as the best available estimate of marginal cost. How might that bias the manager's pricing/output decision?

Let's retreat to production theory to determine how marginal cost relates to average variable cost. If marginal cost is inversely related to marginal product, and if average variable cost is inversely related to average product, similar patterns must arise in costs. Specifically, theory states that

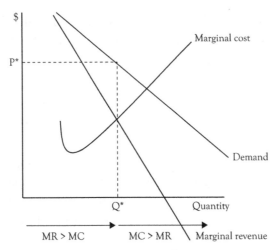

Figure 4.10. Profit-maximizing price and output.

marginal cost should initially decrease with production. Accordingly, average variable cost should fall because decreasing marginal cost brings the
average down. Once diminishing returns sets in, marginal cost will begin
to rise. However, as long as marginal cost is less than average variable cost,
it will continue to pull the average down. Eventually, marginal cost will
exceed average variable cost. Beyond this point, average variable cost
will rise. This implies that average variable cost will be at its lowest level
when marginal cost is equal to average variable cost. This is shown in
Figure 4.11.

Note how average variable cost and marginal cost are identical at only
two output levels (the first unit and Q_{minAVC}). If the cost accounting
method reports average variable cost as its best available proxy for marginal
cost, unit cost will be overestimated for all output levels less than Q_{minAVC}.
This will cause the firm to underproduce and overprice. Similarly, for output
levels exceeding Q_{minAVC}, the estimated proxy for marginal cost (average
variable cost) will be too low. *In this case, the firm will be deluded into
producing too many units and underpricing its production.*

Let's add one more piece to the cost puzzle. Some cost accounting
methods include fixed overhead in their unit cost estimates. This means
that the manager is relying on average total cost as the best estimate of
marginal cost. How might this bias the manager's decisions?

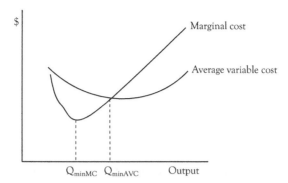

Figure 4.11. Marginal cost and average variable cost.

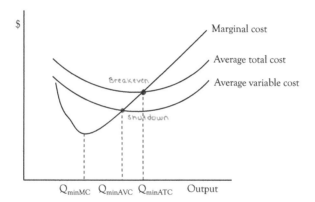

Figure 4.12. Marginal cost, average variable cost, and average total cost.

Earlier, we noted that the average total cost is the sum of the average fixed cost and the average variable cost. If we include the average total cost curve in the illustration, we get the cost curves depicted in Figure 4.12.

As Figure 4.12 indicates, the same basic problem exists with average total cost. According to the figure, marginal cost is less than average total cost for all production levels less than Q_{minATC}, but exceeds average total cost at output levels greater than Q_{minATC}. As with average variable cost, marginal cost is either underestimated or overestimated, leading the manager to either underproduce/overprice or overproduce/underprice.

Step Cost Functions

Earlier, we noted that marginal costs are, by definition, variable costs because fixed costs do not change with production. But if production decisions should be based on marginal costs, and fixed costs are not part of marginal cost, why do some cost accountants use average total cost as their best estimate of marginal cost?

Recall that we can break fixed costs into two categories: **unavoidable fixed costs** and **avoidable fixed costs**. Unavoidable fixed costs will not change if the decision is implemented. For this reason, unavoidable fixed costs are sunk costs and not relevant to production decisions. Avoidable fixed costs are fixed costs that will change if a given decision is implemented. This makes them relevant costs.

Let's use the doughnut shop example to illustrate. The shop paid $1,000/month for rent and purchased a $6,000 fryer capable of making 180 doughnuts per hour. As long as the shop was considering production levels of 180 doughnuts per hour or less, the rent and fryer constitute unavoidable fixed costs because the expenses were unchanged regardless of the output level.

But suppose business had grown to the extent that the shop was capable of selling 250 doughnuts per hour. With only one fryer, it would be incapable of meeting the demand. To meet demand, it would have to purchase a second fryer. Because increasing doughnut production from 180 doughnuts to 250 doughnuts forces the shop to purchase a second fryer, the $6,000 cost of a new fryer is an avoidable fixed cost for any doughnut production exceeding 180/hour. The shop owner would have to determine if the additional doughnut sales justify the additional $6,000 expenditure. If the additional profit contribution is not sufficient to cover the cost of the new fryer, the shop could manage the excess demand by raising the price of the doughnuts.

Let's bring back some of the data from Table 4.10. The $6,000 cost of the first fryer was not relevant to production or pricing decisions because it was an unavoidable fixed cost. But suppose demand has increased, causing Mary to consider buying a second fryer. This makes the cost of the second fryer an avoidable fixed cost that is relevant to the production decision. Let's assume the shop is open eight hours/day, 360 days/year.

Demand is such that 180 doughnuts per hour (518,400/year) can be sold at a price of $.60, and 250 doughnuts/hour (or 720,000/year) can be sold for $.50. The second fryer reduces some of the logjam that exists with one fryer, increasing the workers' marginal products. This would cause the variable cost figures to differ from what appeared in Table 4.10. Let's assume the average variable cost is equal to $.15 at either output level. Can Mary justify buying the second fryer?

Table 4.13 shows the results. As the table indicates, the additional revenue generated as a result of increasing capacity more than covers the relevant costs associated with buying a fryer to increase production.[3]

Let's make a slight adjustment to the table. This time, we will assume the price of the doughnuts will have to fall to $.48 if production increases to 250 doughnuts/hour.

Table 4.14 shows the implications. This time, the relevant revenues are not sufficient to cover the relevant cost. Mary should not purchase the second fryer.

Let's take the analysis from Tables 4.13 and 4.14 and relate them to cost accounting methods. Earlier, we questioned the logic of using average total cost as the best available proxy for marginal cost. Table 4.14 showed that when the variable costs of increasing doughnut production are combined with the cost of the second fryer, the additional revenues generated by

Table 4.13. Purchasing a Second Fryer

Price	Quantity	Total revenue	Relevant revenue	Total variable cost + avoidable fixed cost	Relevant cost
$.60	518,400	$311,040		$77,760	
$.50	720,000	$360,000	$48,960	$114,000	$36,240 → buy fryer

Table 4.14. Another Possibility for the Second Fryer

Price	Quantity	Total revenue	Relevant revenue	Total variable cost + avoidable fixed cost	Relevant cost
$.60	518,400	$311,040		$77,760	
$.48	720,000	$345,600	$34,560	$114,000	$36,240 → do not buy fryer

increasing capacity was not sufficient to cover the relevant costs. But the fryer is an example of fixed overhead. If Mary relied only on average variable costs to make her decision (i.e. she ignored the $6,000 cost of the fryer), the relevant cost in Table 4.14 would be shown as $30,240, misleading her into thinking production should be increased to 250 doughnuts/hour.

Does this imply that Mary should rely on average total cost as the most reliable estimate of marginal cost? Not necessarily. Average variable cost was misleading in this example only because Mary was considering an increase in production that necessitated buying a second fryer. For production decisions that can be accommodated with the existing fryer (180 doughnuts/hour or less), the fryer is an unavoidable fixed cost and is not relevant to production decisions.

If we were to plot the fryer expense, we will uncover a step cost function. The expense of a fryer is fixed until it reaches its capacity. Additional doughnut production requires a second fryer. The expenses associated with two fryers remain unchanged until they are both used to capacity. Beyond 360 doughnuts/hour, the fryer expense bumps up to another level. This is shown in Figure 4.13.

Step cost functions complicate the measurement of unit cost. Within a stairstep, the fryer expense is an unavoidable fixed cost. As we move from one stairstep to another, the expense becomes an avoidable fixed cost. Should unit cost estimates reflect the cost of the fryers? One may take the perspective that because the fryer is not a variable cost, it should not be

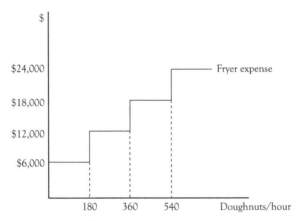

Figure 4.13. Step cost function.

included in unit cost estimates. However, if production increases entail jumping to another stairstep, the fryer is relevant to production decisions. This suggests that including fixed overhead in the unit cost estimate over-states marginal cost within a stairstep, but is a component of marginal cost across stairsteps.

Let's complicate matters even further. In our example, the shop knows the precise production levels associated with the stairsteps. If it limits pro-duction to 180 doughnuts/hour, it needs one fryer. If it wishes to produce 181–360 doughnuts/hour, it needs two fryers. With many firms, the pro-duction levels associated with each stairstep are not known with certainty. Consider a university. The larger the student enrollment, the more faculty members are needed. An additional student does not necessitate an addi-tional faculty member: expanding the class size from 50 students to 51 does not imply a need for more faculty. As enrollments rise, the university may add sections without adding faculty. But eventually, university enroll-ment approaches a stairstep that requires additional faculty. The precise enrollment level associated with each stairstep is unknown; the university only has a general awareness of the ranges of enrollment that might require additional faculty.

Long-Run Costs

The discussion of step cost functions segues into the economic theory of short-run and long-run costs. In some business disciplines, "short run" is explicitly defined, usually as six months or a year. The economic definition of the short run is much more flexible: we define it as the period of time in which there is at least one fixed cost. No fixed cost is indefinite. Mary signed a lease with high hopes of a profitable venture. But suppose the level of demand was less than anticipated. The monthly rent is an unavoid-able fixed cost, but leases expire. Suppose Mary borrowed the funds to buy the fryer and makes monthly payments. If Mary decides to discontinue the business, she will still be obliged to make payments, but eventually the fryer will be paid off. Perhaps she can sell the fryer at some salvage value.

At the other extreme, the business may be so successful that Mary considers opening a second doughnut shop. Or a third. Over the long run, all expenses are either variable or avoidable fixed costs. Economists are reluctant to assign a fixed time frame to what constitutes the "short run" because it will vary by situation. Suppose Mary bought the equipment with cash and signed a year's lease. In that circumstance, one might reasonably conclude the short run is a year. Had she signed a three-year lease, the short run might be defined as three years.

Are long-run costs simply the summation of short-run costs? For example, can Mary assume that the cost of operating three identical shops simply three times the cost of operating one shop?

Theory suggests that this will not be the case in most circumstances. Recall that the law of diminishing returns causes marginal product to fall as inputs are added to production. Increasing the scale of operations may forestall the onset of diminishing returns. For example, as opposed to buying a second fryer, Mary may have considered buying a larger fryer when the shop was first opened. The incremental cost of a large initial fryer may be less than the cost of a second smaller fryer. If so, the average cost of producing 250 doughnuts per hour may be less than the average cost of producing 180 doughnuts/hour. When increases in production lead to decreases in long run average costs, the firm is experiencing ***economies of scale***.

Increasing production does not always lead to economies of scale. Beyond a given point, large-scale production may lead to additional layers of personnel whose efforts may be difficult to coordinate. This may cause long run average costs to rise with production, resulting in ***diseconomies of scale***.

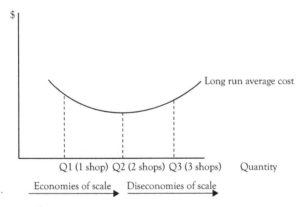

Figure 4.14. Long-run average cost curve.

Economists generally assume that as firms expand their operations over the long run, they experience economies of scale followed by diseconomies of scale. The doughnut shop owner may, for example, find that the average cost associated with two shops is lower than that of one shop, but that the average cost of three shops is higher than that of two shops. This is depicted in Figure 4.14. As the graph shows, the long-run average cost is minimized by operating at Q_2, which corresponds to two doughnut shops. As with any decision, the net benefits or cost of expansion should be determined by identifying its relevant revenues and costs.

Summary

- Economic theory predicts that as inputs are initially added to production, marginal product will rise as the inputs become more specialized. Once the law of diminishing returns sets in, the marginal product of each additional input will fall.
- As long as the marginal product of the additional input exceeds the average product, average product will rise. Once marginal product falls below average product, average product will fall. This means that the average product will rise to a maximum level, but will eventually begin to fall.
- Fixed costs refer to costs that do not vary with production. The average fixed cost will fall as more units are produced. Variable costs are expenses that vary with production. Whereas total variable costs will rise as output increases, average variable cost will initially fall as production increases, but will eventually rise. Total costs begin with the firm's fixed costs and rise as production increases. Average total costs decrease with production initially, but eventually rise.
- Marginal cost is the additional cost generated by an additional unit of output. It falls as marginal product rises, but increases once the law of diminishing returns causes marginal product to fall.
- The firm will maximize profits by producing every unit for which the marginal revenue is greater than the marginal cost. It will lose money on every unit whose marginal cost exceeds its marginal revenue.

- Few firms know the marginal cost of each unit of output. If its cost accounting uses average variable cost as a proxy for marginal cost, the firm may produce too little or too much output. If the firm uses average total cost as a proxy for marginal cost, it will allow fixed costs to influence its production level even though fixed costs are not usually relevant to production decisions.

- Some fixed costs follow step functions. Between discrete ranges of output, these constitute unavoidable fixed costs. At the stairstep, they become avoidable fixed costs. In many instances, the firm does not know with certainty the production level that will necessitate an increase in fixed costs.

- When firms have sufficient time to make changes to overall capacity, theory predicts that firms should initially encounter economies of scale in response to increases in production. This causes average cost to fall. As production continues to rise, the firm eventually faces diseconomies of scale, which causes average costs to rise.

CHAPTER 5

How Accountants Measure Opportunity

The chapters up to this point provide great detail about the decision making process. In particular, we have thus far discussed the theory behind opportunity costs, relevant revenues and costs, demand, and production costs. Up to this point, however, we have only dealt with economic theory. Theoretically speaking, decision makers ideally estimate opportunity costs before making decisions. However, managers in the business world seldom have the luxury of being able to assess true opportunity cost because estimating opportunity costs would require the decision maker to evaluate all possible decisions and determining relevant values for each one. For example, the decision to replace old equipment with new equipment might contain the following possibilities: rebuild or improve existing equipment; purchase new equipment; lease new equipment; or do nothing. Each decision will require a different amount of cash. The differences in cash required can then be used to invest in different projects, pay off debt, hire new employees, or increase inventory or supply reserves. Thus, the process of evaluating all of the possibilities would be extremely c:ostly. As a result, managers often rely upon accounting costs as estimates of opportunity costs in order to save time and money.

Accounting Costs

Accounting costs refer to the amount of cash or other asset that must be sacrificed to obtain some benefit or probable future benefit for a firm. These costs are different from opportunity costs because they are backward looking. That is, accounting costs represent the outcome of previous decisions, whereas opportunity costs represent benefits foregone as the result of future decisions. Accounting costs serve three main purposes. The first purpose is to provide information to external users. This is typically referred to as financial accounting and is governed by Generally Accepted Accounting Principles (GAAP), a set of rules developed by the Financial Accounting Standards Board (FASB). GAAP have evolved to provide information in a manner that best describes the financial events of a company; however, rule makers always face the tradeoff between relevancy and reliability. That is, increasing the level of required reliability may, at the same time, decrease the ability of a company to provide relevant information because accounting data often include estimates. For example, bad debt expense is recorded during the period sales are made even though the company has no way of knowing exactly who will default on their payments. A more reliable way to record bad debt expense would be to wait until the accounts become uncollectable. However, this method would decrease the information's relevancy because it would likely not be available until sometime after the period in which the sales were made, thereby reducing the usefulness of that period's accounting information for investor and creditor decision making.

Within financial accounting, accounting costs are used to describe a company's assets on the balance sheet and expenses on the income statement. The two main principles that exist to guide accounting costs in these areas are the historical cost and the matching principles. The historical cost principle requires accountants to record assets at the original cost. With few exceptions, the cost of the asset remains on the books at the price it was originally purchased.[1] Thus, many companies have land or buildings on their books that have recorded values significantly lower than their fair market value. The matching principle requires the matching of expenses to periods in which the benefits are received. For example, a five-year insurance policy purchased for $5,000 would lead to $1,000 of insurance expense for each of the five years. While this is useful for predicting future cash flows and more clearly reflecting the economic reality to investors and creditors, accrual-based profits and losses are not the same as economic profits and losses. From a decision making view, the timing and amount of cash inflows and outflows is what is important. In the case of the insurance expense, the cash outflow at the beginning of the policy is where the decision maker should focus.

The second purpose accounting costs serve is in tax preparation. Taxes represent a large portion of corporate expenses, potentially eating away almost 40% of a company's profit. Thus, tax-based accounting is a very relevant topic. However, corporate taxes are governed by the Internal Revenue Service Tax Code, which currently has over 72,000 pages. Thus, a discussion of taxes is beyond the scope of this text. The only point worth mentioning concerning taxes is that noncash expenses, such as accounting depreciation can sometimes have cash effects through their impact on tax liabilities.

The third purpose of accounting costs lies in managerial applications. That is, accounting cost data serves to provide managers information useful for making decisions and seeing that those decisions are carried out. Managers of a firm not only have to make decisions based upon the best information available at a given time, but they must also dictate these decisions to others and must make sure those people actually carry out the manager's decisions. Making sure those decisions are carried out is usually referred to as the control aspect of managerial accounting. Control in this sense does not refer to the use of force or manipulation, but rather a state of equilibrium where the employee does what the employer wants because it is in the employee's best interest. An example of this is the firm providing some bonus compensation based upon accounting performance. In this case, employees will try harder to increase performance for the company so that they themselves may earn more money. Although studies show most firms prefer to use accounting information for control purposes, the decision making aspect is also very important, as the decision making step precedes that of the need for control. As such, this chapter will in detail discuss how accounting costs are calculated and how different costing methods can lead to less-than-optimal decisions. In particular, we focus on product costing because it is so important to operations and the accounting methods have a large impact on the costs reported.

Inventory Costs

When a company produces inventory,[2] accountants assign values to the inventory based upon the costs that were incurred to acquire or produce the inventory, not based on its market value or even its replacement value. If a baker was paid $20 an hour to make a cake that had $3 of ingredients in it and it took him 30 minutes to complete the cake, the accountant would say the cake had a cost of $13 ($20/hr × 0.5 hr + $3). Note that these costs represent the costs of an event that has already taken place. That is, accounting costs are backward looking and as such, are not necessarily good for decision making purposes. As mentioned before, this is because the historical cost principle required by the US GAAP requires assets to remain on the books at the costs initially incurred to obtain them.[3] Accounting costs do not disclose the fair value that an item can be sold for, nor do they detail what it would cost to create another item under the present market conditions. Instead, they provide a record of an event that has already taken place. Although accounting costs are backward looking and opportunity costs are always forward looking, production costs are usually consistent over short periods of time. As a result, accounting costs may provide reasonable estimates of the opportunity costs of producing or purchasing the same products in situations when costs do not fluctuate rapidly. Nonetheless, it is always important to be mindful of the differences between accounting and opportunity costs when making decisions.

Let us now consider what is included in the cost of inventory. Accounting rules require any costs necessary to manufacture a unit of inventory to be included in the cost or valuation of inventory. If it cost $20 to produce one desk, then the desk will be included in inventory at $20. To understand this better, however, we must ask what costs are necessary to produce a unit of inventory. Some costs are easier to see than others. In particular, let us return to the doughnut example from Chapter 4. What costs are necessary to produce one doughnut? The easiest cost to see is the cost of the materials that go into the doughnut.

Rather than list the prices for eggs, sugar, milk, flour, and vanilla, let us suppose we have doughnut mix which costs $3 per pound. Additionally, assume one pound of this mix makes 60 doughnuts when water is added. Thus, it is easy to see that the cost of the ingredients for one doughnut is $\frac{\$3}{1\,lb} \times \frac{1\,lb}{60\,donuts} = \$0.05$. This cost represents the material that is required to make one doughnut and is directly traceable to the doughnut, as demonstrated. Materials that are used in producing inventory are called *direct materials*. In addition to the materials, an employee must be paid to mix the batter and put it in the oven. Assume the employee is paid $12 an hour and spends six minutes working on one batch of 60 doughnuts. The cost of that employee is also directly traceable to a doughnut through the same method used for the ingredients. Specifically, each doughnut will require

$$\frac{\$12}{1\,hr} \times \frac{1\,hr}{60\,minutes} \times \frac{6\,minutes}{60\,donuts} = \$0.02$$ of labor. The cost of labor that is

used in the manufacturing process is called *direct labor* because it can be directly traced to the units produced. The cost that is directly attributable to products (direct material and direct labor) together is known as *prime cost.* Thus, the prime cost of one doughnut is $0.07 in total. Although prime costs are the easiest costs of a unit of inventory to determine, they usually do not represent the entire cost of a unit of inventory.

Are direct labor and direct material the only costs necessary to produce a doughnut? No. Many other costs are needed to produce a doughnut. In addition to direct material and direct labor, manufacturing overhead must also be included into the cost of the inventory. *Manufacturing overhead* refers to the cost of indirect labor, indirect material, and factory operating costs used for the production of inventory. These costs are called indirect costs because they cannot be directly traced to the inventory produced and they must instead be allocated. Note that the production of doughnuts would not be possible without them, so the company should include them as a cost of production. The cost incurred to convert raw or direct materials into finished inventory (direct labor and manufacturing overhead together) is known as *conversion cost.*

Indirect costs in the bakery would include the cost of the employee for the time spent cleaning the store or repairing any equipment (indirect labor), the cost of supplies like nonstick solution that is put on baking trays (indirect material), and the cost of electricity, rent, equipment depreciation, and other operating costs (factory operating costs). Assume that these costs amount to $5, on average for every $1 of direct labor cost. In this case, the bakery will allocate $5 of overhead cost to the doughnut for every $1 of direct labor that is traced to the doughnut. Using this ratio, each doughnut

should have $0.10 of overhead ($0.02 direct labor $\times \dfrac{\$5\ \text{overhead}}{\$1\ \text{of direct labor}}$)

allocated to it. The accounting cost to produce one doughnut is $0.17. Remember that only costs necessary for production of inventory are allocated to them. These costs are referred to as *product costs* and only include direct material, direct labor, and manufacturing overhead. Other costs that are necessary for operations, such as sales or marketing costs, are referred to as *period costs* and are not allocated to inventory because they are more attributable to the period in question and not necessary for inventory production.

It is important to distinguish between product costs and period costs because, as mentioned before, US GAAP requires expenses to be matched to the period in which the benefits are received. In the case of inventory, the benefit refers to revenues generated by selling a product. Although period costs are expensed in their entirety during the period in which they are incurred, the matching principle dictates that product costs only be recorded as expenses during the periods in which the products actually sell. This expense is called the **cost of goods sold expense** and it shows up on a company's income statement. The product costs of goods not yet sold remain on the balance sheet as inventory.

Using Accounting-Derived Costs to Make Decisions

Although allocating overhead costs to inventory is useful for conveying the total cost incurred to manufacture a product, it also diminishes the usefulness of inventory costs for decision making. Specifically, accounting costs are problematic because the allocation process requires making estimates at the beginning of the period and because many of the overhead items allocated to inventory are fixed costs and cannot be avoided. Remember that unavoidable fixed costs, such as rent, should not affect the decision of how many units to produce because those costs will be incurred regardless of what level of production is chosen. Consider the following example:

A frame manufacturer produces picture frames. Their frames require $5 of direct material and $1 of direct labor each. In addition to the prime costs, the company also incurs $8,000 of rent and must allocate it via manufacturing overhead per month. Frankie chooses to allocate this cost to the picture frames via direct labor dollars and, based on his estimated level of total production, requires $2.00 of overhead to be allocated to picture frames for each $1 of direct labor. Table 5.1 exhibits the corresponding price/demand table.

Based on Table 5.1, a rational manager would choose to produce 24 units because that level of production results in a profit of $12,800, which is the highest available possibility. Again, though, it is important to stress that including fixed costs, such as rent, into the decision making process is not a good way to make decisions because fixed costs will not vary with changes in production level. This point is well made by excluding the overhead portion from Table 5.1. Doing so results in Table 5.2.

Based on this table, the company should produce 850 frames and sell them for $23 each. Which table is correct? The overhead (rent, in this case) incurred must be paid for regardless of how the company chooses to prepare its accounting records. Costs that do not vary among choices are not relevant costs and should not be included in the decision making process. Thus, the correct choice is to produce and sell 850 frames for $23 each. Recall from Chapter 3 that demand increases as price decreases. At some

Table 5.1. Firm Profit Schedule

Price	Demand	Cost	Total revenue	Total cost	Profit
$20	1,000	$8	$20,000	$8,000	$12,000
21	950	8	19,950	7,600	12,350
22	900	8	19,800	7,200	12,600
23	850	8	19,550	6,800	12,750
24	800	8	19,200	6,400	12,800
25	750	8	18,750	6,000	12,750
26	700	8	18,200	5,600	12,600

WITH $2 OH

Table 5.2. Firm Profit Schedule

Price	Demand	Cost	Total revenue	Total cost	Profit
$20	1,000	$6	$20,000	$6,000	$14,000
21	950	6	19,950	5,700	14,250
22	900	6	19,800	5,400	14,400
23	850	6	19,550	5,100	14,450
24	800	6	19,200	4,800	14,400
25	750	6	18,750	4,500	14,250
26	700	6	18,200	4,200	14,000

Without $2 OH

point, the additional revenue from selling more units is overcome by the decreases in contribution margin. Due to the overestimation of unit costs, this point is reached more quickly so managers decide to sell fewer units. The result is that fewer units are sold at too high of a price and the company makes $50 less ($14,450 – 14,400). Thus, it should be clear that accounting decisions can have a real impact on firm performance.

Allocating production costs to inventory is required per US GAAP for financial reporting purposes and it is important for properly reflecting economic reality to investors and creditors. Excluding these costs would imply costs of goods sold were lower than they really were and would result in an inflated gross profit. The demonstration above clearly showed how including fixed overhead in the cost of production can potentially lead to less-than optimal decisions being made with respect to price-production schedules. That notwithstanding, the allocation of fixed costs is sometimes used as a control mechanism. Let us consider when it might be desirable to allocate fixed costs.

Taxing Externalities

The benefit of cost allocations is that they affect behavior, allowing firms to curb specific behaviors that results in negative externalities. **Externalities** are consequences (either benefits or costs) that are experienced by parties not directly related to the decision. For example, acid rain was a negative externality when manufacturers released sulfur dioxide and nitrogen oxides into the atmosphere. The effects of poisoned water sources and eroded structure surfaces were experienced by parties completely unrelated to the release of those pollutants into the air. In contrast, the increase in neighborhood property value that results from a resident landscaping his or her yard is an example of a positive externality. Although the neighbor bore the full cost, the other parties benefited.

The problem with externalities is that the party whose activities generate the externality doesn't factor them into his decision. For example, a person who decides to get a flu shot weighs the benefit of the shot (reducing the likelihood of contracting the flu) against the costs (the money and time involved in getting the shot). Should he get the shot, other persons also benefit to the extent that they will not contract the flu bug from him.

But it is unlikely that the cost/benefit analysis he undertakes includes the benefits to those he comes in contact with.

Negative externalities entail a similar dilemma. In this case, the party's action imposes an external cost on a third party. Anvil Farms in Boxford, Massachusetts uses bone gel, a byproduct of gelatin made from cattle bones, to fertilize its fields. Unfortunately, the fertilizer emits an odor so noxious that local residents complained to the Board of Health.[4] Beyond being a nuisance, the odor might conceivably reduce the property value of homes within its range. The problem is that Anvil Farms makes its decision based on its own revenues and costs, not those imposed on neighboring residents.

The economic solution to negative externalities is to force decision makers to incur the costs they would otherwise ignore. London, England initiated congestion pricing in its Central Business District in 2003 to reduce traffic congestion. When driving into the city during peak hours, drivers consider only their own personal costs and benefits. The notion that their decision to drive into the city adds one more car for other drivers to contend with is generally ignored. To force drivers to incur this cost, the city imposed a congestion charge. Cars entering Central London on weekdays between 7 am and 6:30 pm must pay a fee of £8. Video cameras installed throughout the city record license plate numbers and match them against the list of those who paid for the privilege. Violators are fined £40.[5]

The philosophy is that forcing drivers to incur the congestion charge will cause them to consider public transportation as a way to get downtown or to avoid driving into the city during peak hours if it can be avoided. Indeed, after the charge was implemented, traffic decreased by 20%, or 20,000 vehicles/day while bus and subway ridership increased by 14% and 1%, respectively.

Applying the concept to corporations, decisions at the factory level are made by weighing revenues against costs, given that factory supervisors are often rewarded for the profitability of their facility. But production decisions can impose costs on other departments. As long as these costs are borne by outside parties, the plant supervisor has no incentive to consider them. In such circumstances, the supervisor may overproduce the good, increasing the profitability of the plant, but decreasing that of the firm.

A common example with corporations is the allocation of the Human Resources department to departments and then to the products those departments produce. This cost is a relevant production cost because the HR department supports the direct labor force. The cost of the HR department follows a step function as described in Chapter 4. That is, the HR department can only serve a certain number of employees before it must hire additional staff. Between discrete numbers of employees, the HR costs are fixed, and hence, unavoidable. Once the HR department is at maximum capacity and a stairstep point is reached, the additional costs required to hire more employees are avoidable fixed costs.

Just because HR expenses do not rise between stairsteps doesn't mean there is no negative externality incurred by hiring an additional employee at the plant. Rather, the impact of increasing the number of employees is felt in HR even though its expenses do not rise. That is, the quality of service provided by HR suffers because the additional work must now be covered by the same staff. In fact, it is because the effects are felt that HR decides it needs to add to its personnel. This decrease in quality or higher cost is the externality that companies try to mitigate. Assuming the cost of the HR department represents a significant portion of the overhead, allocating overhead based on some measure of direct labor could be beneficial. By allocating overhead with direct labor hours, management is inclined to use fewer employees. More specifically, allocating the HR department's cost based on the use of employees actually captures a portion of the opportunity cost of hiring an additional employee. To consider it in another light, imagine the department using employees does not get charged for the HR department. This acts as a discount on the total cost of production, so management from this department would overconsume economic resources through the use of labor. Allocating overhead costs based on a measure of direct labor should result in less direct labor being used. Using less direct labor should result in a lower cost for the Human Resources department. Thus, allocating costs could produce the desired outcome.

Allocating overhead acts as a tax and therefore reduces whatever behavior it is linked to. As pointed out above, this is sometimes useful in approximating the opportunity cost of using a cost driver and reducing the overconsumption of resources. However, the reduction of consumption can sometimes be too large and may result in a much worse overall position than would occur in the absence of cost allocation. The cost of adding one more employee does not increase the costs of the HR department neces-sarily. After adding enough employees, though, it does become necessary to add another HR representative.

When to Allocate Costs

If possible, it is desirable to allocate costs at their marginal rates, as this method would lead to the most efficient decisions that would be based on real economic costs. Unfortunately, this method is not feasible due to its complexity and the high costs that would have to be incurred to do so. The allocation of costs, instead must rely upon average costs, which are very seldom equal to marginal costs. Thus, the allocation of costs is either done so at a rate that is lower than or higher than marginal costs. When costs are allocated a rate lower than marginal costs, overconsumption is still reduced, just not at the optimal level. A tax that is lower than the marginal rate still decreases consumption of whatever is being taxed, which is ben-eficial to the company. In contrast, allocating costs when the allocation rate is higher than the marginal rate will result in too much reduction of con-sumption. This is especially true if external sources of replacement exist. That is, when the allocated rates are higher than marginal costs, managers will reduce consumption by an amount that is larger than desired. This reduction results in the same fixed costs being spread among a smaller allocation base, which leads to an even higher allocation rate. Again, more managers will reduce consumption of the allocation base. This process continues until the rate is so high that no consumption of the allocation base occurs. This phenomenon is known as a *death spiral.* The takeaway from this is that allocating costs are beneficial from a control standpoint when the allocation rate (average cost) is less than the marginal cost.[6] Consider the example from a wood company below.

Table 5.3. Product Profit Report

	Desk	Chair	Table
Revenue	$100,000	$200,000	$150,000
Variable cost	$70,000	$120,000	$90,000
Fixed cost	$50,000	$50,000	$50,000
Profit	($20,000)	$30,000	$10,000

Table 5.4. Product Profit Report without Desk

	Chair	Table
Revenue	$200,000	$150,000
Variable cost	$120,000	$90,000
Fixed cost	$75,000	$75,000
Profit	$5,000	($15,000)

Tables 5.3 and 5.4 illustrate the death spiral. In Table 5.3, the fixed costs are distributed evenly between the three products. Looking only at the profit, the conclusion would be to drop desks from production. Discontinuing desks requires the entire $150,000 of fixed costs to be allocated only to chairs and tables. The profit analysis resulting from this decision is included in Table 5.4. As before, looking at the profit analysis suggests producing tables is unprofitable.

After dropping the tables from production, chairs must absorb the entire $150,000. Producing and selling only chairs will result in a total loss of $70,000 ($200,000 − 120,000 − 150,000). Thus, making decisions based on costs that include fixed portions has led a company from profit to loss. Take note that this example does not imply spreading fixed costs over a larger number of products is what makes the company more profitable. Rather, the company is more profitable when producing both chairs and tables because each has a positive contribution margin.

Turning back to the use of accounting costs for decision-making purposes, let us now consider the specific ways accountants calculate inventory costs and how each of these methods can affect the decision made. The three most common methods used to calculate product costs include the absorption, variable, and activity-based costing (ABC). Of these three methods, absorption costing is the only one that is fully allowed under GAAP. As such, we will first discuss this method for determining the cost of a unit of inventory.

US GAAP requires all costs necessary for the production of a unit of inventory to be included in the cost of that unit of inventory. These costs include those that are easily traceable to inventory, such as direct materials and direct labor. They also include the costs that are more difficult to link to a specific unit of inventory, such as the cost of maintenance, janitorial staff, supervisors, and the human resources and accounting departments.[7] This second group of costs is referred to as manufacturing overhead and includes all costs necessary for producing inventory that are not direct material or direct labor. These costs include costs for indirect labor, indirect materials, and factory operating costs. As mentioned before, they must be allocated because they cannot be directly traced to each unit produced.

Absorption costing allocates overhead based upon volume of input, not output. That is, the overhead is allocated based upon something that is required to produce overhead rather than dividing overhead by the total number of output. The benefit to using an input rate is it allows companies to allocate overhead during the period via a predetermined overhead rate as opposed to waiting until the end of the period and retrospectively allocating costs. For example, a company has a good idea of what the utility bill will be at the beginning of the month, but they may not actually know what the bill is until the end of the month. Using the actual overhead incurred would require waiting until the end of the period to allocate overhead. Another benefit of using predetermined overhead rates is that costs often fluctuate around some average. These fluctuations are typically small and balance themselves out most of the time so using a predetermined rate provides a consistent cost. A last reason for using units of input rather than output for allocating overhead is that companies produce more than one type of product and these different products require different amounts of prime costs and overhead costs. Using the number of products produced to allocate overhead would certainly undercost a complicated product that takes several steps to produce, while at the same time overcosting products that are simple and quick to make.

Based on unit cost

Under absorption costing, companies try to choose a unit of input for allocating overhead that is most positively related to the level of overhead. That is, managers of a firm want to as accurately as possible allocate the costs to the units that are producing those costs. If the largest part of overhead comes from machine maintenance or depreciation, then allocating overhead based on machine hours is a logical choice. If the largest portion of overhead comes from having more administration costs to handle all of the direct laborers, then using direct labor hours is probably a good choice. The choice of input is usually limited to machine hours, direct labor hours, direct labor dollars, and direct material dollars. Whichever allocation base a company chooses, it is important to note the allocation of overhead acts as a tax. As described before, the increased cost associated with one more unit of input will make using that unit of input less desirable. To the extent that the input mixes are already at their optimal ratio preallocation, any allocation of costs will shift the input mix away from that point.

For example, a chemical company has several divisions. One of those divisions, Chemicals 1, produces Product X using various chemicals. Chemicals 1 can make Product X using two different solutions that require different amounts of labor to mix. The labor responsible for mixing the units is paid $20 per hour. The production cost schedule is presented in Table 5.5.

According to Table 5.5, Solution A should be used to produce batches of Product X, as it has a lower overall cost by $1,000. If fixed costs are allocated at a rate of $10 per direct labor hour, the new cost schedule is as shown in Table 5.6.

According to the cost schedule in Table 5.6, Solution B should be used because total costs are lower by $3,000. Despite the increased fixed costs allocated due to a higher number of labor hours, the actual fixed cost has not increased. Thus, the result of choosing Solution B will actually still

Table 5.5. Production Cost Schedule

	Solution A	Solution B
Material cost per batch	$8,000	$15,000
Labor hours required to process	1,600	1,200
Labor cost per hour	$15	$15
Total cost per batch	$32,000	$33,000

Table 5.6. Production Cost Schedule with Fixed Costs

	Solution A	Solution B
Material cost per batch	$8,000	$15,000
Labor hours required to process	1,600	1,200
Labor cost per hour	$15	$15
Allocated fixed cost per hour	$10	$10
Total cost per batch	$48,000	$45,000

result in a higher cost by $1,000, leading to lower profits for the company as a whole. As this example shows, the allocation of costs can lead to less than optimal results.

Absorption Costing   Fixed OH is a unit cost

With all of that said, let us now discuss the process used to actually allocate the overhead. The first step is to estimate the amount of overhead that will be incurred during the period. This process usually involves examining prior period overhead and working with various budgets to determine how much will be consumed during the current period. The next step is to determine which measure of input is most highly correlated with the levels of overhead and choose it as the allocation basis. Finally, estimate the quantity of input that will be used. The predetermined overhead rate, as it is called, is then calculated as

$$\text{Predetermined overhead rate} = \frac{\text{Estimated overhead}}{\text{Estimated quantity allocation base}}$$

Overhead is then allocated to units during the period as the units of input are used. For example, Foster Glass Company specializes in making glass mugs. At the beginning of 2013, Foster estimates it will have $2,000,000 of fixed manufacturing overhead during the period and chooses to allocate it based upon machine hours. Foster expects to have one million machine hours during the period, which means the predetermined overhead rate will be $2 of overhead for every one machine hour used on a job $\left(\frac{\$2,000,000}{1,000,000 \text{ MH}}\right)$. On average, it takes 0.05 machine hours to produce a standard glass mug. This translates to $0.10 of overhead allocated to each glass mug ($2 × 0.05).

Estimated Overhead

Estimated Quantity

    The amount of overhead applied over a period almost always differs from the actual amount of overhead incurred during a period because the amount of overhead is based on estimates. Consider the following example:

    Assume a company manufactures two types of products, the T3 and T4 models. This company estimates it will have $1,400,000 of overhead for the period and will allocate this overhead using direct labor dollars as the allocation base.

Table 5.7. Production Cost Information

Product	Annual volume	Direct labor per unit	Direct material per unit
T3	5,000	$40.00	$150.00
T4	10,000	$50.00	$200.00

Table 5.7 summarizes the estimated production and cost data for the two products. Based on this information, we calculate the predetermined overhead rate as the total estimated overhead divided by the total estimated allocation base, which is $\dfrac{\$1,400,000}{(5,000 \times \$40)+(10,000 \times 50)} =$ $\dfrac{\$1,400,000}{\$200,000 + \$500,000} = \$2$ of overhead per $1 of direct labor. If the

(Direct Labor)

company incurs $250,000 of direct labor expense relating to the production of 5,500 T3s and $490,000 of direct labor expense relating to the production of 10,000 T4s, how much overhead will be allocated during the period?

To determine how much overhead is allocated, we multiply the predetermined overhead rate ($2 overhead per $1 direct labor) by the actual amount of allocation base used ($250,000 for T3 and $490,000 for T4). This calculation indicates $500,000 of overhead will be allocated to T3 units and $980,000 will be allocated to T4 units. The total overhead allocated during the year is $1.48 million. During the period only $1,450,000 was actually spent on overhead. This results in a $30,000 difference between actual and allocated overhead. The difference can be handled in three ways. Most commonly, the difference is adjusted away through the cost of goods sold expense account. In this case, cost of goods sold would be decreased by $30,000 because too much overhead had been allocated to the units, most of which presumably sold. The second way to handle the difference is by reallocating the over/under allocated to the various inventory accounts based on the amount of overhead that is already in the works in process, finished goods, and cost of goods sold accounts.

For example, if the company has ending inventory balances of $29,600, $59,200, and $1,391,200 in its work in process, finished goods,

Table 5.8. Overhead Reallocation

	Work in process	Finished goods	Cost of goods sold
Overhead allocated	$29,600	$59,200	$1,391,200
Percentage of overhead allocated	2%	4%	94%
Overhead prorated	($600)	($1,200)	($28,200)
Ending overhead	$29,000	$58,000	$1,363,000

and cost of goods sold accounts respectively, then the treatment of the overallocated overhead would be as shown in Table 5.8.

Notice the account balances are reduced because the actual overhead is less than the company previously assigned during the period. Also, note that the accounts that had the most allocated overhead experiences the highest amount of change. Finally, the last way to account for the difference in allocated and actual overhead is to recompute a retrospective overhead rate based upon actual overhead incurred and the actual allocation base. After calculating the actual overhead rate, use it to apply the accurate amount of overhead to various products during the period. This method is not often used because it is backward looking and requires more work than it is worth. The most common method is to adjust the cost of goods sold account for the difference between allocated and actual overhead.

Although absorption costing is required by US GAAP, it is criticized by many for two main reasons. The first reason is that it creates an incentive to overproduce inventory. Recall that the costs of direct materials, direct labor, variable overhead, and fixed overhead are all included in inventory as product costs. These costs then either go to the income statement through cost of goods sold expense or they remain on the books as ending inventory.

Producing more overhead than can be sold reduces the amount of fixed overhead included in each unit because the fixed cost allocation is done through average costs. The variable costs (direct labor, direct material, and variable overhead) remain relatively constant for each unit produced, but the fixed portion of the product cost decreases with each additional unit produced. By producing more units than can be sold, a portion of the fixed overhead is allocated to the units that remain in ending inventory. Thus, fixed overhead costs that are necessary for

The more produced, the lower OH cost

producing a normal level of production are hidden in ending inventory, resulting in a lower cost of goods sold and a higher income for the period. Although the cost of goods sold is lower for the period, the fixed costs must still be paid. Thus, the only difference is in how the accounting records report the costs. Additionally, overproduction for the sole purpose of reducing per unit costs presents a case of wasted resources. The variable costs require cash outlays resulting in foregone investments in other projects.

Consider the following cost information for 2013 (Table 5.9):

Table 5.9. Inventory Cost Data

Operating data for 2013	
Units produced	120,000
Unit sales	100,000
Material cost/unit produced	$0.40 per unit
Labor cost/unit produced	0.30
Fixed overhead/unit produced	0.20
Variable overhead/unit produced	0.10

There is no beginning inventory and the company sells 100,000 units at $5 per unit. The absorption costing method results in a product cost of $1 for each unit ($0.4 + 0.3 + 0.2 + 0.1). In this case, income is 100,000 × $5 per unit minus 100,000 × $1 = $400,000. Notice how they produced 20,000 more units than they sold. This overproduction results in allocating $4,000 of fixed overhead away from the units sold in 2013 to the ending inventory. Again, the fixed overhead costs are still incurred, but the accounting expenses will be deferred until the next period when it will be recognized as the inventory is sold. Several motivations exist for this behavior, but two stand out as most likely. First, most managers receive bonuses based upon some form of accounting earnings. Second, increasing earnings for the period may help the company obtain cheaper debt financing or raise more capital through stock issuances. Thus, managers may very well likely have incentives to overproduce inventory.

Variable Costing

Fixed OH is a period expense

In response to the overproduction problem created by absorption costing, many firms maintain a second set of internal books for calculating period-based income. This method is referred to as variable costing because it only includes variable costs as product costs. Direct materials, direct labor, and variable overhead are all included in product costs, but fixed overhead is treated as a period expense instead. Period expenses are expensed when they are used or expire, in contrast to product expenses, which are only expensed when inventory is sold. This mitigates the incentive for managers to overproduce because the extra units of inventory no longer absorb a portion of the fixed overhead. However, the variable costing method is not allowed for financial reporting purposes because it does not adhere to the matching principal. Maintaining multiple sets of books creates additional expenses for firms and creates the possibility of mistakes. In practice, about 22% of firms use variable costing.[8] In addition to problems from multiple sets of books, variable costing also introduces the issue of who gets to choose which costs are variable and which costs are fixed. Although this decision is fairly straightforward for most costs like rent and repairs, some costs are more difficult to determine (depreciation, utilities, etc.).

Consider the information from Table 5.9 again. Under the variable costing method, the fixed costs are expensed in whichever period they are produced. Specifically, using variable costing would result in income of 100,000 × $5 per unit minus 100,000 × $0.8 and 120,000 × 0.2 = $396,000. The company produces 120,000 units and only sells 100,000 regardless of which method is chosen. The difference is purely one of accounting. However, the $4,000 of income is still important. Using variable costing provides better data for managers to make pricing decisions. It allows managers to more appropriately assess the profitability of product lines. The number of units produced and sold varies significantly between periods. Variable costing allows managers freedom from biases in costing data based on a predetermined overhead rate that may not be accurate depending on how well estimated allocation base and actual allocation base usage align.

Nonetheless, variable costing still has weaknesses. First, variable costing produces unit costs that are more in line with marginal costs, but still rely upon historical costs. Accounting costs by nature will always represent the outcomes of previous decisions and should be carefully evaluated before being used as a basis for future decisions. Furthermore, variable costing does away with the benefit of allocating fixed costs to proxy for opportunity costs. Assuming a company is in an environment where resources are constrained, the fixed cost allocation can serve a tax to reduce consumption of scarce resources. From a control point of view, there are other ways to reduce managers' desire to over overproduce inventory. A few examples of alternative techniques include applying a holding charge for inventory based on the firm's cost of capital, basing managements' compensation on stock performance if the firm is publicly traded, and stipulating bonuses are only paid when inventory levels are below a certain threshold.

Perhaps a more important concern, as far as decision making goes, is that absorption costing can produce inaccurate product costs. Most companies use a measure of direct labor or direct material to allocate overhead; however, costs can vary with other measures (e.g. machine setups). When firms set machines up for new runs, they often record the labor costs for the setup, but do not note the actual number of setups or what their cause was. Allocating costs based on one measure alone (e.g. direct labor hours) presents a problem because it does not distinguish between products or departments that have low volume and multiple setups or complicated production processes and products or departments with high volume and few setups or simple production processes.

Consider two paint producing plants. The first Plant, Plant W, produces gallons of white paint that comes in different finishes (e.g. flat or satin). This Plant produces 100,000 gallon batches before switching between finishes. The second plant, Plant C, produces white Paint in similar finishes, but also produces the colored paint that is added to white paint in department stores to give the consumer the color he or she wants. Plant C produces 100,000 gallon batches of white paint and 5,000 gallon batches of various colored paints before switching products. Two-thirds of the output from Plant C is white paint with the remainder being colored paint. Plant C has higher overhead costs than Plant W because its employees must spend more time cleaning the vats used to produce paint and setting them up for the different runs. Although most of the output from plant C is white paint, the bulk of the differences between overhead costs in the two plants is due to the smaller batches of colored paint.

Recall, however, that absorption costing allocates overhead based upon a measure of input, such as direct labor or direct material. The result of this allocation method is that white paint in Plant C will capture approximately two-thirds of the overhead. Thus, the cost of white paint from Plant C will be higher than that in Plant W despite the extra costs being the result of the colored paint. An upper level manager considering this data may make two mistakes. The first mistake would be to discontinue the white paint production at Plant C because it can be produced cheaper elsewhere. Notice that this decision would not avoid most of the overhead costs. Instead it would transfer them to the colored paints. The second mistake a manager might make based on this information is to overproduce color paint and sell it at a very low price, failing to recognize the true costs of its production.

Activity-Based Costing

To resolve this issue, some firms have implemented what is called activity-based costing (ABC). In contrast to absorption costing's use of a single allocation base, ABC assigns indirect costs to separate pools based on what drives their costs and then allocates these costs to products based on the level of activities used in production. Rather than costing activities varying solely with changes in production volume, they are now able to correspond to changes at the unit, batch, product, and facility level. Separating activities into these four levels allows a firm to more accurately assign costs to those products that are driving them.

As the names suggest, unit-level activities are activities, such as assembly processes, that are performed each time one unit of a product is produced. These costs would include utilities associated with the production process (electricity to power the equipment). Batch-level activities include activities that take place each time a new batch is produced and include activities such as machine setups and material handling. Product-level activities are activities that take place in support of particular product lines. Costs that are required for each product line produced include design, modification, creation of instruction manuals, and technical support. Lastly, facility-level activities take place to support the entire facility. This level of activity includes items such as insurance, building depreciation, rent, property taxes, plant maintenance, utility costs incurred not directly related to the production process, and human resources. After tracing costs to the different activities, overhead rates are calculated for each activity and then assigned to the products or jobs based on the amount of activity it takes to produce a unit or to complete the job.

The following provides an example to compare ABC with traditional absorption costing. Suppose a security company produces the following three security systems: simple, advanced, and ultimate. During the year this company produces 60,000 simple, 30,000 advanced, and 10,000 ultimate security systems. The total estimated overhead costs for the period was $8,290,000. This cost consisted of depreciation, research and development, quality assurance, machine setups, and supporting staff salary. Table 5.10 shows the costing information available for the period.

Using this information, we obtain the following application rates by dividing the cost pool by the amount of cost driver, as shown in Table 5.11.

Under ABC, the application rates are then used to allocate the indirect costs to the three specific products. The resulting costs are reported in Table 5.12.

Finally, the cost per unit of each security system is calculated by dividing the total cost for the units by the number of units produced. The results are reported in Table 5.13.

Table 5.10. Cost Information

	Estimated costs	Cost driver	Estimated usage of cost driver
Depreciation	$2,000,000	Per sq ft	40,000
R&D	3,000,000	Per product	3
Quality assurance	990,000	Per inspection	220
Machine setups	1,800,000	Per setup	450
Supporting salary	500,000	Per direct labor hour	200,000

Table 5.11. Activity-Based Costing Overhead Rates

Activity		Application rate
Depreciation	$2,000,000/40,000	$50 per sq ft
R&D	$3,000,000/3	$1,000,000 per product
Quality assurance	$990,000/220	$4,500 per inspection
Machine setups	$1,800,000/450	$4,000 per setup
Supervisor salary	$500,000/200,000	$2.5 per direct labor hour

Thus, using ABC results in product costs of $52, 84, and 265 for the simple, advanced, and ultimate security systems respectively. These costs of production are more accurate than if traditional absorption costing had been used because each cost is allocated based on a specific activity that drives the cost.

Using traditional absorption costing and direct labor hours as an allocation base results in an overhead rate of $\frac{\$8,290,000}{200,000 \text{ DLH}} = \$41.45$ per direct labor hour. Multiplying this rate by the total direct labor hours results in the cost statistics shown in Table 5.14.

Thus, using a traditional absorption-based costing system results in each security system costing $82.90 regardless of whether it is simple, advanced, or ultimate. This simple example is used to illustrate the point that absorption-based costing sometimes results in inaccurate product costs. If the company based its pricing and production decisions upon the absorption-based costs, they would likely try to sell too few simple security systems because its price would be set too high. Not only would this have the result in lower profits initially, but it would ultimately lead to a death spiral because they would produce fewer simple units, thereby increasing the costs of the advanced and ultimate units. Eventually, the company could cease production entirely. Again, this is an extreme example, but the underlying principle holds true.

If ABC is so much better than absorption-based costing and for understanding costs, making decisions, and evaluating performance, then why don't all firms use it? It seems complexity is a double-edged sword for ABC. The first problem with ABC is that it takes time to set the system up. Someone must go through a company's production process and

Table 5.12. Inventory Cost Analysis

Activity	Depreciation	R&D	Quality assurance	Machine setups	Supporting staff salary	Total cost
Application Rate	$50 per sq ft	$1,000,000 per product	$4,500 per inspection	$4,000 per setup	$2.5 per direct labor hour	
Usage for simple	15,000	1	60	200	120,000	
Cost for simple	$750,000	1,000,000	270,000	800,000	300,000	$3,120,000
Usage for advanced	10,000	1	60	150	60,000	
Cost for advanced	$500,000	1,000,000	270,000	600,000	150,000	$2,520,000
Usage for ultimate	20,000	1	100	100	20,000	
Cost for ultimate	$750,000	1,000,000	450,000	400,000	50,000	$2,650,000

Table 5.13. Total cost for inventories

	Total cost	Quantity	Cost per unit
Simple	$3,120,000	60,000	$52
Advanced	$2,520,000	30,000	$84
Ultimate	$2,650,000	10,000	$265

Table 5.14. Traditional Absorption Costing

	Direct labor hours	Cost per DLH	Total cost	Quantity	Cost per unit
Simple	120,000	$41.45	4,974,000	60,000	$82.9
Advanced	60,000	41.45	2,487,000	30,000	82.9
Ultimate	20,000	41.45	829,000	10,000	82.9

determine where all the costs come from and what drives them. This process is both tedious and is partially subjective. That is, department managers may resist allocating costs to activities their departments use considerably. After determining what the costs are and what drives them, additional data on these cost drivers must also be maintained. To capture this data, a firm may have to implement new accounting and information technology systems. Staff will also need to be trained for the new systems. Implementing an ABC system is costly; however, that is not the only issue. Even after establishing an ABC system, the system itself may provide too much information. As more information is produced, the value of each piece of information produced decreases because management may have a difficult time focusing on what is important. Also, the differences between ABC and absorption costing are usually only significant for products that are produced in small quantities at a time. Thus, the benefit for many firms is simply not enough to justify the additional costs incurred to implement and maintain the system. Along this line, research shows that ABC does not have a significant impact on operating performance.[9] Finally, ABC many times does not adhere to US GAAP because the systems are designed to include nonmanufacturing costs, such as customer support.

When making decisions it is extremely important to be mindful of the fact that accounting costs represent historic costs regardless of the costing method used. Accounting data is important for making decisions because opportunity costs are not usually readily available. However, accounting costs are only useful for making decisions to the extent that they approximate opportunity or marginal costs.

Summary

- Accounting costs are historical in nature and primarily reflect the results of a previous decision. Historical data is useful for evaluating performance, but is helpful in making decisions to the extent that it estimates opportunity cost.
- Product costs include everything necessary to produce a unit of inventory. These costs include portions of fixed overhead, which do not vary with changes in production volume. Including fixed costs in product costs results in less than optimal production-pricing decisions.
- Fixed cost allocations are sometimes useful when curbing overconsumption or undesirable behaviors.
- Traditional absorption-based accounting allocates overhead costs based on units of input. This results in costs being averaged over production volumes, creating an incentive to overproduce so that a portion of fixed costs will remain in ending inventory rather than being included in cost of goods sold.
- To mitigate managers incentive to overproduce inventory, some firms use a variable costing system that expenses all fixed overhead costs in the period they are incurred. This system must be maintained as a supplemental system because it violates the matching principle and cannot be used for financial statement purposes.
- Absorption-based costing also produces inaccurate product costs because overhead is assigned to units based on volume and not on what actually drives the overhead costs. To compensate for this, some firms have instituted ABC systems. These systems trace overhead costs to products through the activities that drive them.

- ABC systems are expensive and complicated to implement and maintain. As a result, most firms have either not implemented them, or have implemented them and returned to traditional absorption-based systems.
- Regardless of the method used to calculate inventory costs, it is important to be mindful that these costs are historical by nature and that opportunity costs are always forward looking.

CHAPTER 6

Are You a Better Decision Maker . . . Yet?

Ultimately, the success of a manager boils down to how well he applies economic concepts to his decisions. Ironically, our observations seem to indicate that managers often rise through the ranks of companies without fully understanding the basic economic tenets of decision making. It isn't that they are bad at their jobs; in fact, the opposite is usually true. Most firms only promote the most productive employees. But successful managers make their way up the corporate ladder not just because they're hardworking or understand company politics. Rather, the successful manager is willing to question convention and think outside the box.

Let's illustrate through a real-world example. Donald Washkewicz became chief executive of Parker Hannifin Corporation in 2001. Throughout its history, the firm employed simple cost-plus pricing techniques for its 800,000 products. The managers would calculate the cost of producing the item and tack on 35% as a markup. And why not? It's simple, straightforward, and the firm had been doing it this way for years.

But Washkewicz was not convinced that the "tried-and-true" way to set prices was necessarily the best way. His new system separated each product into one of five categories, based largely on the price elasticity of demand. At one end of the spectrum were the core products that were produced in high volumes and subject to intense market competition. At the opposite extreme were products that were custom-designed for specific customers or otherwise available only through Parker Hannifin. Rather than mark each product up by a fixed percentage over unit cost, prices were set in accordance with the price sensitivity of buyers. As a result of the new approach to pricing, the firm's profits soared from $130 million to $673 million in only five years.[1]

Washkewicz may not have consulted a microeconomics textbook when he changed his firm's pricing strategy, but the results are consistent with the economic theory of the firm. If a manager uses economic theory as the foundation for making decisions, more often than not, the right decision will be made.

In writing this book, our goal is to help managers make better decisions. Let's reflect on the past five chapters as a guide to decision-making. Our first major point was that each decision must add to the value of the firm. This means that the relevant revenue from each decision must exceed its relevant cost. Relevant revenues and costs are those that will change if the decision is implemented.

The extent to which revenues will change can be characterized by demand theory. As the price rises, fewer units will be sold. However, the rate at which consumers respond to price increases is determined by the price elasticity of demand. Until Donald Washkewicz revolutionized pricing at Parker Hannifin, prices were set in accordance with unit cost, not on the basis of demand. By separating the products into categories, Parker was able to set prices based on elasticities.

Demand analysis suggests other factors that ought to be considered by managers. One is potential price effects. It is too easy to equate relevant revenues to the revenues generated by the additional units produced and sold. But will increasing production place downward pressures on the prices of all units? If so, the relevant revenues will be less than originally estimated. In some cases, the firm can set a price for one cluster of customers without changing the price for other customers.[2] In these circumstances, the revenue from the additional units is the relevant revenue and there are no price effects.

The cross-price elasticity of demand measures the sensitivity of unit sales for one good to changes in the prices of related goods. Few firms produce exactly one product. Quite often, the firm's product lines include goods that are complementary or substitutes. Changing the price of one good will affect the unit sales of related goods. Managers need to be cognizant as to how pricing decisions affect all related products.

Chapters 4 and 5 help managers anticipate relevant costs. But measuring relevant cost is far more challenging than the concept implies. Relevant cost is, by definition, a measure of the opportunity cost of implementing the decision. But as we discussed in Chapter 5, accounting costs often differ from opportunity costs. Accounting costs are historical by nature whereas opportunity costs are always forward-looking. To the extent that accounting costs captured opportunity costs in the past and opportunity costs have not changed, then accounting costs will continue to capture opportunity costs. Otherwise, they are not the same.

Another difference between accounting and opportunity costs can be quite problematic. Chapter 4 demonstrated that unless a decision incurs avoidable fixed costs, relevant cost is the same as marginal cost. The economic theory of cost demonstrates that each unit of production has its own unique marginal cost. Although the marginal cost decreases initially, once the law of diminishing returns sets in, the marginal cost of each unit steadily rises.

But it would be prohibitively expensive for a cost accountant to be able to measure the cost of producing each individual unit. Consequently, cost accounting measures of unit cost are invariably based on averages. If the firm employs variable costing, only variable costs are reported as unit cost. But the reported figure is average variable cost, not marginal cost. Alternatively, absorption costing applies variable costs that are traced to products over short periods of production, as well as fixed costs that are allocated to products based on various cost drivers. In this case, the reported unit cost estimate is average total cost, which, again, is not the same as marginal cost. Activity-based costing is simply a more sophisticated way to allocate overhead on the basis of cost drivers; specifically, each activity is assumed to have its own cost driver. Nonetheless, because fixed overhead is allocated to individual units of production, the resulting unit cost estimate is average total cost, not marginal cost.

Does this really matter or is the distinction merely semantic? Theory suggests that marginal cost is rarely the same as average total or average variable cost. Therefore, if relevant cost is marginal cost, and the unit cost estimates are not the same as marginal cost, then the manager is in a position to make bad decisions. Failing to understand the difference between marginal cost and unit cost estimates can lead to producing too much or too little output and setting less than optimal prices.

While one might think this is acceptable over the long haul because the differences between marginal and average costs balance out over time, the distinction can actually be quite problematic. The problems arise because some projects with understated opportunity costs are chosen when they should not be. Similarly, some projects with overstated opportunity costs are dismissed when they should have been accepted. Thus, the company loses money whether opportunity costs are over or understated.

Rockwell International once became concerned with the erratic sales performance of its heavy-duty truck axles. By closely examining their costing practices, which routinely allocated overhead on the basis of direct labor hours, the firm realized it was overestimating the unit cost of its high-volume axles by 20% while underestimating the cost of the other axles by as much as 40%.[3] Because prices were based on unit cost estimates, Rockwell set prices for the high-volume axles that allowed competitors to freely enter the market.

This does not imply accounting costs are without merit. Estimating opportunity costs can be extremely costly and accounting costs serve as a more affordable benchmark to use when making decisions. Additionally, many accountants use different methods to record accounting costs to try to compensate for some of the problems inherent to accounting based product costs. As discussed in Chapter Five, these methods all have their strengths and weaknesses.

So how can a manager use the information in this book to make better decisions? Here are a few practical steps that can be taken. The first step is rather simple: dive deeper into the data and ask questions. Oftentimes, the individuals who provide the data have some economic sense, but they see their job as providing the figures, not explaining or decomposing them. Ask the accountants who provide the cost information what is included and whether these costs are relevant to the decision. Ask whether the costs provided include any fixed costs that do not vary with changes in production volume. If the answer is yes, then those costs should be removed for a more accurate examination. Ask the marketing people how intense is the level of price competition and the degree to which prospective buyers can find adequate substitutes. Ask the finance people how the cost of capital was determined and what role it should play in the final project analysis.

Consider the following simple example. A local restaurant owner was considering whether he should purchase radio advertising. Based on local market characteristics and previous results, his marketing group concluded that advertising on the radio would increase his restaurant's sales by 12%. The cost of radio advertisement was more than 12% of his profits, so he concluded it was not worth the investment. After some discussion, however, he soon realized that many of the costs included in his profit were fixed costs and would not increase with the changes in sales (e.g. rent, electricity, insurance, depreciation, and others). After excluding the fixed costs, the restaurant owner determined the increase in profit from extra sales far outweighed the cost of the advertising. Thus, asking questions, diving deeper into the data, and re-examining the costs with fixed costs removed is generally the first step.

If the accountant or other people who are providing you data are unable to provide sufficient insight as to what should be done or which costs do not vary, the second step is to ask what accounting method was used to determine the costs. Regardless of which method is used, it is important to remember that accounting costs are historical by nature and that things change over time. Thus, you should make sure the accounting costs presented are still consistent with current production cost estimates. If the production costs have changed, then the current cost estimates should be used rather than the historical accounting costs. Additionally, it is important to remember that accounting costs do not capture marginal costs because they are based on average costs. Nonetheless, more accurate cost data can be calculated in certain situations if it is deemed necessary. This more accurate data will still be based on averages, but it will be closer to the relevant cost figure.[4]

One last point inherent to all product costs is that allocated fixed costs may be beneficial because they can reflect negative externalities. That is, some of the allocations may capture the opportunity costs of strained supporting roles (e.g. janitorial, human resources, and others). Our suggestion is to eliminate fixed costs when making decisions, but this should be tempered by the caution to consider any effects decisions may have on supporting services.

After determining which costing method has been used, the following steps should be taken. If the absorption costing method is used, then fixed costs have been allocated to product costs and should be backed out before considering which price and production levels net the maximum profit. Although fixed costs are very important in terms of profitability, they are irrelevant when making decisions because they are fixed and do not vary between the available choices (assuming they are unavoidable, which is the case when examining product costs). Remember that you are only concerned with relevant costs and that these costs only include costs that vary between decisions. If the variable costing method is used to determine product costs, then fixed costs do not have to be backed out. Nonetheless, you still need to be mindful of the points discussed earlier. Finally, if activity-based costing is used, fixed costs have once again been allocated to product costs and should be removed before making a specific choice.

If you still feel uncomfortable or uncertain making a substantial decision after reading the first five chapters of this book and following the steps described earlier, then our last bit of advice is to consult with an external source. Many firms have the necessary staff in place to provide consulting internally. In the event that you do not have staff available to provide the correct guidance internally, the decision is of significant importance to your business, and you still feel uncomfortable making the decision based upon the knowledge you gained from reading this book, you may want to hire a professional consultant. Most cities have firms that specialize in consulting. You should contact a certified public accountant if you cannot find a firm that specializes in consulting. People are usually hesitant to hire consultants because the consulting cost represents an additional expense. However, making incorrect decisions also lowers profit. Hence, you may find that the benefits from hiring a consultant more than justify the costs. This book was written to help the business community benefit by explaining how to make better business decisions using economic theory and an understanding of how accounting costs are calculated. It is our hope that this book has and will continue to serve you well.

APPENDIX I

Advantages and Disadvantages of Various Cost Accounting Methods

Cost accounting method	Description	Advantages	Disadvantages
Absorption	Variable and fixed manufacturing overhead are allocated to inventory units based on measures of input (e.g. direct labor hours).	Simple implementation and supported by GAAP.	Stores fixed costs in ending inventory and inaccurate product costs.
Variable	Only variable manufacturing overhead is included in inventory costs. Fixed overhead costs are treated as period expenses.	Does not hide fixed overhead costs in ending inventory.	Not supported by GAAP and ignores externalities.
Activity based	Both variable and fixed overhead costs are allocated to inventory based on measures of activity (e.g. set ups, teardowns).	Results in most accurate product costs.	May not be allowed under GAAP and is costly to use.

APPENDIX II

Relevant Published Case Studies

Available through Harvard Business Publishing:

1. The Springfield Nor'Easters: Maximizing Revenues in the Minor Leagues
2. Netflix: The Public Relations Box Office Flop
3. Superior Manufacturing Company
4. Catawba Industrial Company
5. Relevant Costs and Revenues
6. Salem Telephone Company
7. Landau Company
8. G. Wilson and Company, Inc.
9. Birch Paper Co.
10. Bridgeton Industries
11. Destin Brass Products Co.
12. Kanthal, Precision Worldwide, Inc.
13. Prestige Telephone Company
14. Wilkerson Company

Notes

Chapter 1

1. Mercator Minerals (2012).
2. Welch (2006).
3. We are assuming no further decline in customer traffic over the next several months.
4. Welch (2006).

Chapter 2

1. Sometimes these are referred to as "incremental" revenues and costs.
2. Unless, of course, the boxes were extremely large!
3. We are assuming that "other" expenses do not vary with the number of boxes sold.
4. Healy and Palepu (2003).
5. We are assuming the promotional expenses have already been incurred. The group may have set a budget of $300, but may decide how much to spend as the fundraiser draws nearer. Any portion that is unspent, but may be spent is avoidable; any portion that has been committed to, but cannot be recovered is unavoidable.

Chapter 3

1. Woo (2011).
2. Welch (2001).
3. Energy Information Administration (2011).
4. Dietz (2008).
5. Welsh (2011).
6. Peoples (2009).

Chapter 4

1. We should note that the positive correlation between labor hours and total product has its limits. Given the limited workspace, it is possible that too many workers would result in congestion and decrease total output. We will not consider that possibility because no firm would commit to hiring too many workers.

2. The fryer, proofer, glazing table, and re-furbishing expenses are also fixed costs. Because they are sunk and not relevant to any future decision, we will focus only on the monthly rent, as it is relevant to the decision as to whether to remain open for business each month.

3. We should note that the table only included the relevant revenue and cost for a year. If the relevant cost for a year exceeded the relevant revenue, Mary would need to consider the useful life of the second fryer in her analysis. To make the analysis as simple as possible, we will assume a useful life of one year with no salvage value.

Chapter 5

1. Long-lived assets are depreciated over their expected useful lives. This depreciation is used to spread an expense over the periods in which a company will receive benefits from the purchase. The depreciation does not accurately relate to changes in fair value, often leading to book values that differ significantly from fair values.

2. Although the accounting and decision making are similar for service, retailers, and manufacturing firms, we limit our discussion to the manufacturing setting because the discussion of accounting practices is easier to extrapolate from manufacturing firms to the others than vice versa.

3. GAAP does allow companies to decrease the value of assets if their perceived value declines below their book value. However, companies are not allowed to increase the book values, unless substantial repairs or improvements have been made.

4. Lewis (2010).

5. Litman (2011).

6. A rule that requires the comparison of average costs to marginal costs is not very useful if marginal costs are unknown. However, Chapter 4 described the relationships between costs. From that discussion, we know that average costs are increasing when they are less than marginal costs. Similarly, average costs decrease when they are higher than marginal costs. Thus, the rule can be reinterpreted as being "allocate costs when average costs are increasing, not when they are decreasing."

7. Factory administration expenses are included in overhead; however, corporate-level administration expenses are not.
8. Hughes & Paulson Gjerde (2003).
9. Ittner, Lanen, & Larcker (2002).

Chapter 6

1. Aeppel (2007).
2. See Marburger (2012a) for a comprehensive discussion of innovative pricing strategies. Additionally, Marburger (2012b) provides insights on the factors that determine market power and proactive strategies to maintain one's position in the marketplace.
3. Worthy (1987).
4. As an example, see the hourly doughnut shop problem discussed in Tables 4.8 and 4.9 in Chapter 4.

References

Aeppel, T. (2007). Seeking perfect prices. CEO tears up the rules. *Wall Street Journal*. Retrieved April 7, 2013, from http://online.wsj.com/article/SB117496231213149938.html

Dietz, K. (2008). How to outpace the industry in snack sales and profit growth. Retrieved December 28, 2011, from National Association of Convenience Stores: http://www.nacsonline.com/NACS/Resources/NACS%20Show%20Handouts /2008/How%20to%20Outpace%20the%20Industry%20in%20Snack %20Sales%20and%20Profit%20Growth.pdf

Healy, P., & Palepu, K. (2003). The fall of enron. *Journal of Economic Perspectives 17*(2), 3–26.

Hughes, S. B., & Paulson Gjerde, K. A. (2003). Do different cost systems make a difference? *Management Accounting Quarterly 5*, 45–55.

Ittner, W., Lanen, N., & Larcker, D. (2002). The association between activity-based costing and manufacturing performance. *Journal of Accounting Research 40*, 711–726.

Lewis, B. (2010). Smelly fertilizer peeves neighbors. Retrieved January 18, 2013, from Wicked Local: http://www.wickedlocal.com/boxford/news/x41621046/ Smelly-fertilizer-peeves-neighbors#axzz2IMx0Wsqj

Litman, T. (2011). London congestion pricing: Implications for other cities. Retrieved January 18, 2013, from Victoria Transport Policy Institute: http://www.vtpi.org/london.pdf

Marburger, D. (2012a). *Innovative pricing strategies to increase profits*. New York: Business Expert Press

Marburger, D. (2012b). *How strong is your firm's competitive advantage?* New York: Business Expert Press.

Mattioli, D. (2012). On Orbitz, Mac users steered to pricier hotels. Retrieved September 4, 2012, from The Wall Street Journal: http://online.wsj.com/ article/SB10001424052702304458604577488822667325882.html

Mercator Minerals (2012). Mercator Minerals announces updated El Pilar feasibility study results. Retrieved September 12, 2012, from Marketwire: http:// www.marketwire.com/press-release/mercator-minerals-announces-updated-el -pilar-feasibility-study-results-tsx-ml-1696778.htm

Peoples, G. (2009). iTunes price change hurt some rankings. Retrieved May 22, 2012 from Billboard: http://www.billboard.biz/bbbiz/content_display/industry/ news/e3i7917210cb575a9b91b4543e3d671922a

Welch, G. (2006). Indian Mall struggling. *Jonesboro Sun 103*(153), 1.

Welsh, J. (2011). Hybrid sales surge as gas prices march upward. Retrieved December 31, 2011, from *The Wall Street Journal*: http://blogs.wsj.com/drivers-seat/2011/04/06/hybrid-sales-surge-as-gas-prices-march-upward

Welch, L. (2001). McCallum starts probe of gas price gougers. Retrieved December 20, 2012, from Madison.com: http://host.madison.com/article_b28f92be-c74a-11e0-b76d-001cc4c002e0.html

Woo, S. (2011). Under fire, Netflix unwinds DVD plan. Retrieved September 4, 2012, from *The Wall Street Journal*: http://online.wsj.com/article/SB10001424052970203499704576622674082410578.html

Worthy, F. (1987). "Accounting bores you? Wake up" *Fortune*. Retrieved April 7, 2013, from Fortune: http://money.cnn.com/magazines/fortune/fortune_archive/1987/10/12/69666/index.htm

Zimmerman, J. L. (1979). The costs and benefits of cost allocation. *Accounting Review 54*, 504–21.

Index

R
Relevant costs, 13–24, 23, 104
Relevant revenues, 13–24, 104
  cross-price elasticity of demand,
    43–45
  factors that change demand, 31–32
  law of demand, 25–31
  price elasticity of demand, 33–43

S
Step cost functions, 68–71
Sunk costs, 16, 19, 47

T
Tax-based accounting, 77
Taxes, 76–77
Taxing externalities, 82–85
Total fixed cost, 54–55

Total product, 50
Total variable cost, 54–55. *See also*
    Variable costing
Traditional absorption costing, 97,
    99. *See also* Absorption costing
Tried-and-true way to set prices, 103

U
Unavoidable fixed costs, 23, 24, 68.
    See also Fixed costs
Unitary elasticity, 37
Unit cost, 4, 20, 22, 47, 48
Utility, 26

V
Variable costing, 23, 24, 93–95, 108
  average variable cost, 55–59, 67
  total variable cost, 54–55

OTHER TITLES IN OUR ECONOMICS COLLECTION

Philip Romero, The University of Oregon and Jeffrey Edwards,
North Carolina A&T State University, Collection Editors

- *Managerial Economics: Concepts and Principles* by Donald N. Stengel
- *Your Macroeconomic Edge: Investing Strategies for the Post-Recession World* by Philip J. Romero
- *Working with Economic Indicators: Interpretation and Sources* by Donald N. Stengel and Priscilla Chaffe-Stengel
- *Innovative Pricing Strategies to Increase Profits* by Daniel Marburger
- *Regression for Economics* by Shahdad Naghshpour
- *Statistics for Economics* by Shahdad Naghshpour
- *How Strong Is Your Firm's Competitive Advantage?* by Daniel Marburger
- *A Primer on Microeconomics* by Thomas Beveridge
- *Game Theory: Anticipating Reactions for Winning Actions* by Mark L. Burkey
- *A Primer on Macroeconomics* by Thomas Beveridge
- *International Economics: Understanding the Forces of Globalization for Managers* by Paul Torelli
- *Recovering from the Global Financial Crisis: Achieving Financial Stability in Times of Uncertainty* by Marianne Ojo

Announcing the Business Expert Press Digital Library

Concise E-books Business Students
Need for Classroom and Research

This book can also be purchased in an e-book collection by your library as
- a one-time purchase,
- that is owned forever,
- allows for simultaneous readers,
- has no restrictions on printing, and
- can be downloaded as PDFs from within the library community.

Our digital library collections are a great solution to beat the rising cost of textbooks. e-books can be loaded into their course management systems or onto student's e-book readers.

The **Business Expert Press** digital libraries are very affordable, with no obligation to buy in future years. For more information, please visit **www.businessexpertpress.com/librarians**. To set up a trial in the United States, please contact **Adam Chesler** at *adam.chesler@ businessexpertpress.com* for all other regions, contact **Nicole Lee** at *nicole.lee@igroupnet.com*.

CPSIA information can be obtained at www.ICGtesting.com
Printed in the USA
BVOW11s0949200814

363358BV00006B/17/P